RF^s

STEVE FENNELL

RF184 at Bushey Church.
(London Transport)

ISBN 0 9509910 5 8

Published by DPR Marketing & Sales (The World of Transport),
37 Heath Road, Twickenham, Middlesex TW1 4AW

Printed by The Ludo Press Ltd, London SW18 3DG

CONTENTS

TITLES IN THE SERIES
No. 1 The Routemaster (out of print)
No. 2 London Trolleybuses
No. 3 The RFs
Further titles to follow

Front cover upper: **RF510 is seen at Weybridge Station during the last days of Central RF operation.** *(Steve Fennell)*

Front cover lower: **National Green liveried RF546 is seen at Harefield. Relatively few examples were repainted in this lighter shade.** *(Mike Harris)*

Rear cover upper: **Newly modernised RF201 is seen at Hampton Court on route 725.** *(Geoff Rixon)*

Rear cover lower: **History is made at Kingston Garage in the early hours of 31st March 1979. RF507 has just completed the final public journey of all to be undertaken by a Central RF. The vehicle was restored as much as possible to pre-1965 condition.** *(Steve Fennell)*

INTRODUCTION

It is hard to believe that back in 1951, when the first RFs were delivered, these buses were not universally appreciated! Many considered the new RF to be featureless and boxlike, so unlike the many much admired pre-war vehicles that the RF had replaced. At this stage perhaps it would be wise to acknowledge that the average enthusiast generally does not appreciate the wind of change. Even less so in fact when standardisation is the end result. The 1950's enthusiast, having seen all of his precious pre-war double deck vehicles replaced by a new standardised fleet of RTs, now had to sit back and watch the same sequence of events take place within London's single deck fleet. No wonder the RFs were treated with disdain!

Regardless of personal loyalties, the late 1950's London Bus scene was a sight to behold. Standardisation with all its many advantages could be seen everyday. Everywhere one looked could be seen RTs or RFs. It was a situation that the then London Transport Board had set its sights on before the Second World War and was a mammoth task involving as it did the construction and delivery of almost 8,000 vehicles. The RT and RF and latterly the RM portrayed all that was best about London Transport; sadly those days have gone forever and it is fairly safe to assume that we shall never see their like again!

At the time of delivery the RF was the heaviest two axle single deck service bus ever built, perhaps even the heaviest of all time, and critics voiced opinions that this type of vehicle was obsolete before it was ever delivered. Perhaps in an effort to silence these 'Transport Experts' LT evaluated a number of the new lightweight vehicles that manufacturers were producing in the early 1950s. Hardly surprising was the fact that none found favour within London although many provincial operators took delivery of these new lighter, and as a result of the different form of construction, cheaper vehicles. What isn't widely stated is that the RF outlived all of them; what's more with very little alteration to its original construction. The last RFs in London operated as late as March 1979 and very few people who witnessed the last rites on that March evening would have stated that the RFs running in for the last time that night were time expired. Indeed, RF operation may well have lasted a few years longer had it not been for the insistence of Surrey County Council that larger vehicles on a reduced frequency were far more suited to the county coffers than the service previously provided.

The pages of this book tell the story of London RFs from start to finish with all their many variations over the years. At first glance it might appear that a certain bias towards the Country area fleet is apparent and although not intential it has to be said that more pages are given over to the Green fleet than to those making up the fleet of the Central area. The reason for this is quite simply that more happened to these vehicles than was the case of the red liveried examples. For instance, the Green Line fleet was expanded and subsequently modernised, whilst in later years coaches, both modernised and unmodernised, were converted to buses. In 1970 the formation of London Country Bus Services Ltd produced a myriad of different liveries on the survivors. In contrast the Central fleet underwent two livery changes and conversion to OPO format and basically that was that!

Today, many RFs have ended up in the hands of preservationists and at most Rallies, particularly in the South of England, a considerable number of these vehicles always make an appearance. So prolific is the supply of RFs that sometimes you could be forgiven for thinking that you are in fact at Kingston Garage than at a venue specialising in all forms of preserved PSVs! Although, thanks to the efforts of preservationists, RFs may still be seen in their former glory, never again will there be an atmosphere of years gone by when such buses were taken for granted by many thousands of people throughout the former LT operating area.

STEVE FENNELL

I would like to thank the many photographers who have supplied material for this publication, particularly Alan Cross who provided much of the early material included within at very short notice. Whilst thanks are also due to Peter Graves without whom the statistical information would have been sadly lacking.

UMP227

By the early 1950s London Transport's post-war vehicle renewal programme was well under way as regards the double deck fleet but many ageing pre-war single deckers were still putting in sterling service day after day, patiently awaiting their turn for replacement. The renewal of the single deck fleet had been deliberately delayed by the London Transport Executive who, rightly or wrongly, regarded replacement of the double deck fleet as first priority.

It had always been the intention to apply the same high level of standardisation to the post-war single deck fleet as was being incorporated into the new RT double deck buses being delivered at the time. The problem facing the Executive was as to just what sort of bus would be suitable for the job in hand. The decision had already been reached that a full frontal design with underfloor engine thereby maximising passenger accommodation would be the most suitable. New vehicles of this style had been constructed by the Birmingham & Midland Motor Omnibus Company from 1946 onwards and great interest was taken by the LTE in this project. Consequently in 1949 an approach was made to AECs at Southall for a similar style of vehicle to be made available as a demonstrator. The resulting bus carried 36-seat Park Royal bodywork bearing the registration number of UMP227. Livery was standard London Transport Country area Lincoln Green and Cream. In common with the new RT family vehicles being delivered at the time, an air operated four speed preselector gearbox was fitted. After thorough examination and pre-service testing 'UMP' was allocated to St Albans Garage from May 1950 and trialled on route 355, remaining there until September 1951 when the vehicle returned off loan to AECs. 'UMPs' future seems not to have been well documented under the auspices of AEC but it is known that various development work was carried out using the bus as a testbed.

Soon after the trials with 'UMP' commenced it was announced that an order had been placed with AECs and MCCW for a standardised fleet of 700 single deck vehicles. The post-war single deck vehicle replacement programme was about to begin.

UMP227 is seen at St Albans in July 1950 whilst undergoing evaluation on route 355. The running number carried (SA17) appears to be painted on to the vehicle! Today 'UMP' is part of the collection of the London Bus Preservation Group. *(Alan Cross)*

THE PRIVATE HIRE RFs

The first RFs to be delivered comprised the Private Hire batch, numbered RF1–25. These were the only RFs to be constructed to a length of 27'6'', the remainder being built to the new legal maximum of 30'0''. Deliveries commenced in April 1951 when RFs 1–5 and 7 were taken into stock. Livery was an attractive Lincoln Green and Grey with red lining, fleetnames and numbers. Cant windows were also fitted, this being another feature unique to this batch. Initial allocations were to the following garages: three each to Holloway, Middle Row, Streatham and Upton Park, four each to Merton and Riverside and five to Camberwell. Little changed within the PH RF fleet, the vehicles undertaking duties for which they were intended and additionally being used on guided tours, Hampton Court and Hatfield House being two such popular destinations. However, from February 1954 their first overhaul programme commenced. In those days the concept of body changing at overhaul on RFs had not yet started and the vehicles were overhauled as complete units. About this time a livery change was effected although it is thought that the first examples to receive overhauls retained their attractive green and grey livery. Subsequent vehicles were outshopped in all-over Lincoln Green but retaining the red fleetnames and numbers originally carried.

By the end of 1955 the Green Line fleet was hard pushed to cover all commitments and accordingly ten of the PH RFs were transferred on to Green Line duties. The vehicles concerned were spasmodically drawn from the whole batch but shortly after was standardised to take in the 16–25 series thereby forming a complete batch. The vehicles operated in Private Hire livery whilst being utilised on Green Line and it wasn't until the following year that they were repainted into full Green Line colours and fitted with interior luggage racks, whilst at the same time receiving provision for side roof mounted route boards as standard on the remainder of the Green Line fleet.

The balance of the PH RFs were retained for their former duties but as resources became hard pushed to cover normal service mileage so the amount of private hire and touring work undertaken diminished. By December 1963 the whole batch (including the Green Line examples) were delicensed and put up for disposal. All were gone by February 1964, mostly to independent operators to whom these vehicles gave many further years of excellent service.

The Private Hire RF's shorter length can be clearly seen in this view of RF3 at Hampton Court Vrow Walk in summer 1953. The vehicle is being utilised on one of London Transport's then popular day tours. Just try parking a coach in Vrow Walk today! (Geoff Rixon)

Norbiton Garage plays host to RF14. The vehicle carries the original livery of Lincoln Green and Grey wth Red fleetnames, etc. Arguably the most attractive livery ever to be carried by an RF. *(Geoff Rixon)*

RFs 7 and 25 are seen at High Beach in the heart of Epping Forest. There appears to be some sort of problem with RF25 however judging by the attention that is being given. All the Private Hire RFs were fitted with semaphore indicators when new. *(C. Carter)*

Victoria Gillingham Street Garage acquired a PH RF allocation towards the end of 1954. No doubt the garage's location having some bearing on this decision. RF24 is seen within the confines of the garage, displaying blinds for another of London Transport's popular day tours. *(Author's Collection)*

At first overhaul the majority of PH RFs lost their attractive green and grey livery and were outshopped in all-over Lincoln Green but retained red fleetnames. Compared to their previous colours this scheme looked particularly dreary as can be seen with this line up at Marylebone Station. From left to right are RF12, 5, 14 and 2. *(DPR Collection)*

RF13 has by now received 'dog's-ear' indicators as it pulls away from Wembley Empire Pool in a view estimated to have been photographed about May 1961. *(Author's Collection)*

The LT official photograph of a Private Hire RF in full Green Line regalia. Note that the vehicle retains its semaphore indicators, seen just behind the saloon entrance.
(London Transport Museum)

The interior of a Private Hire RF after Green Line conversion. The luggage racks are an addition concurrent with revised status. Seat moquette was identical to that employed on production Green Line RFs.
(London Transport Museum)

RF23, in full Green Line guise, is seen at Eccleston Bridge, Victoria on route 719. The use of PH RFs on Green Line work was intended to be a stop-gap and the intention was that they would always be the first to be withdrawn once replacements were available. Nevertheless, their spell of Green Line operation lasted almost six years. *(G. Mead)*

Route 703 had not long to last when this view of RF17 was taken. LT's own electrification of the adjacent Metropolitan 'Underground' Line taking what little traffic remained. *(P. J. Relf)*

A most unusual operation was the use of RF16 on local bus work from Stevenage Garage in November 1959. The vehicle is seen on route 383 at Hitchin. *(H. W. Peers)*

THE RFWs

Following on after the delivery of the PH RFs came a batch of 15 luxury coaches which were classified RFW. The 'W' incidentally standing for 'wide' as these vehicles were constructed on a 8'0" version of the standard RF chassis. Length being to the new legal maximum of 30'0". These vehicles were very advanced for their time and featured extensive areas of glazing. Full drop windows and two sliding roof sections were fitted and each of the 39 seats was provided with its own independent reading lamp. Most unusually bodywork was by Eastern Coach Works, a situation initiated by the Government who were pressurising London Transport to make use of this newly nationalised manufacturer. Livery carried was identical to that of the private hire RFs recently delivered. Garages to receive an initial allocation of these vehicles were Dalston (3), Old Kent Road (3), Northfleet (1), Putney Chelverton Road (3), Reigate (1), Romford (2), Watford Leavesden Road (1) and Windsor (1). These vehicles met the same fate as the PH RFs, the continuing staff shortage effectively curtailing the private hire operations. By October 1964 the whole batch of 15 were delicensed and offered for disposal. Whilst a small number found their way into the fleets of independents, the vast majority were sold to the Ceylon Transport Board, the only RF variants to be disposed of abroad. Of those that remained in this country, two examples have been obtained by preservationists.

Ostensibly on a 'London Airport Tour' is RFW15 seen at Victoria. Semaphore indicators were originally fitted to this class, their position can be made out just behind the headlights. *(Gerald Mead)*

RFW12 poses for the photographer in Cornwall Road Bus Stand, Waterloo. The RFWs were difficult vehicles to track down and photograph as one never quite knew where they would turn up. *(Gerald Mead)*

The plush interior of an RFW. Seat moquette utilised was the same styling as that carried by Private Hire and Green Line RFs. *(London Transport Museum)*

The RFWs led uneventful lives as Touring and Private Hire vehicles. RFW1 is seen at Epsom Downs on the occasion of the 1953 Derby . It appears to be picnic time in the foreground, with one member of the party either suffering from over indulgence or attempting to make an indepth study of the underside of an RFW! *(Geoff Rixon)*

Hampton Court is still a popular venue for excursionists although today most appear to favour the private car! RFW14 keeps the company of what appear to be Bedford OBs in this summer 1953 view taken at Hampton Court. *(Geoff Rixon)*

THE GREEN LINE RFs

RF26 –288: *Original Build.*

RF289–294: *Converted from Central buses in March 1956.*

RF295–313: *Converted from Country buses in March 1956.*
Vehicles renumbered from RF514-516, 697, 518-532 respectively
(original 295-313 renumbered 514-532).

The Green Line RFs were the first in the fleet to be built to the then new legal maximum length of 30'0''. Externally the livery featured considerably more Lincoln Green than on previous Green Line vehicles. The only relief being a lighter band of green on the moulded window surrounds. Internally the coaches carried 39 deep foam well spaced seats, one of which on the offside faced inwards, whilst luggage racks, saloon heaters and air-operated doors were fitted as standard.

RF26 was delivered in September 1951 and the following month entered service from Tunbridge Wells Garage on route 704. Deliveries were rapid and by the year's end 109 examples had arrived. As 1952 dawned so deliveries increased and by July the vast majority of the Green Line fleet had been updated. The final trickle of vehicles arrived by October, by which time attention had turned to the construction of the Central area batch. (For a full list of route allocations see Appendix F.)

Initially, there were few changes to the sphere of operation of these fine vehicles but by 1954 a serious shortage of Green Line RFs was apparent. This was in no way attributable to their mechanical capabilities but was the result of an expanding network. From July 1953 the new South Orbital 725 route had been introduced which had placed a severe strain on resources whilst the number of duplicates that were now scheduled had far exceeded the stock of RFs that were available. In fact so desperate was the shortage that a number of standard Bus RFs were standing in as coach spares while their place on bus work was taken by some of the displaced 10T10s relegated by Coach RFs in the first place.

So as to replace the 10T10s, and to allow Coach RFs to be used as coach spares, it was decided that the entire RF allocation at Grays, operated on routes 723/A, would be removed in favour of a batch of new RTs painted in full Green Line livery but retaining their bus interiors, a case of mutton being dressed as lamb if ever there was one! The 24 surplus RFs indirectly obliterated the 10T10s from the schedules, allowing a suitable quantity of coach spares, and enabled the introduction of a new service, the 720A, allocated to Epping Garage.

Although this allowed a temporary reprieve, the Green Line fleet's insatiable appetite for RFs continued. The development of the New Towns surrounding London was in full swing and traffic was on the increase. As yet, road congestion and railway modernisation had yet to have any impact on the standard of service provided, and further means of expanding the Green Line fleet were being considered. As a result at the end of the 1955 summer season ten of the shorter Private Hire RFs were loaned to the Green Line fleet. Initially, RFs 3, 5, 7, 11, 12, 15, 17, 19, 21 and 22 were allocated, operating in the second PH livery of all over green with red fleetnames and numbers. From December, however, RFs 3, 5, 7, 11, 12 and 15 were returned to PH duties and their place taken by RFs 16, 18, 20, 23, 24 and 25, making an inclusive batch from 16–25. Still the demand for vehicles was not met and commencing in February 1956 a more radical approach was adopted.

Between February and April 1956 25 RFs were drawn from the Central and Country Area fleets and converted to Green Line Coaches. At the same time a large scale renumbering of part of the fleet was effected so as to keep different types of RF in their respective batches. RFs 289–294 were taken from the Central fleet and were converted to Coach status. Initially, all that this involved was a repaint into the relevant livery and the fitting of platform doors (Central buses at this time were 'open platform'). The other 19 RFs so converted were drawn from the Country Bus fleet and as platform doors were already fitted all that was initially involved was a repaint. The vehicles concerned were RFs 514–6, 697 and 518–32 and these were renumbered to RFs 295–313 respectively. (The original 295–313 were renumbered 514–532.) RF517 was deliberately omitted from the batch as it was one of the original OPO format buses which was renumbered 697, more of which in the Country Bus section. After this batch of vehicles had been dealt with it was the turn of the ten ex-PH RFs to receive the attentions of the paintshop. These received full Green Line livery between April and June 1956 as well as mounting brackets and hooks so as to receive Green Line side route boards. Internally, luggage racks were fitted. Further attention was afforded to the 289–313 batch of RFs at overhaul between January and May 1957. This involved the fitment of the mounting brackets and hooks for the side route boards whilst internally luggage racks, heaters and new flooring were fitted. The seating was rearranged but, due to the bus spacing of the frames, one extra seat above that of a standard Green Line RF was obtained. This taking the form of an offside inward facing double seat at the front instead of a single as on production coaches. Suffice to say that these 25 vehicles somehow lacked the character of the production build. In particular the luggage racks always appeared to be 'add-on extras' which indeed they were. Coupled with the fact that even after overhaul they retained bus seating squabs their original status was never really disguised. Nevertheless, they served a useful purpose for some considerable time even though the conversion of the first six (289–294) managed to cause a Trade Union dispute as a result! More details of which will be found in the Central Bus section.

The Green Line fleet now settled into a period of relative stability. Heater modifications were effected to the whole fleet commencing from September 1957 and whilst this was undertaken RFs 17, 26, 41, 125, 304 and 309 were used as float vehicles acting as cover where required. The stability within the Green Line fleet was not matched by the Country Bus RFs which were being converted to permit driver only operation. It had been decided that a few bus routes

The updating of the Green Line fleet was extremely rapid and in little under twelve months a total of 263 Coach RFs had been delivered. Many routes benefited from such an influx of vehicles as standardisation was applied to the single deck fleet. RF178 shares the forecourt of Dorking Garage with C25 whose turn for replacement would have to wait a few months later. *(Geoff Rixon)*

justified the provision of crew single deckers but because the only vehicles available were RFs these had been provided even though they were equipped for OPO. From June 1959 the spare Coach RFs (i.e. special duplicates and late running spares, etc.) were replaced by RTs. The displaced crew operated Coach RFs being allocated to the bus routes where crew operation was to be retained and the OPO fitted Bus RFs were released to effect economies elsewhere. The routes which received these Coach RFs were the 391 (St Albans), 406C and 447 (Reigate) and 458 (Windsor). This was the first time that Green Line RFs had been allocated to bus work, although odd appearances and 'bus before coach' workings had occurred in the past.

In August 1960 16 RFs were outshopped in a new lighter green livery. The vehicles concerned (RFs 33, 36, 41, 42, 51, 52, 55, 58, 69, 71, 72, 86, 126, 271, 309 and 313) were all allocated to either High Wycombe or Reigate Garages for use on route 711. The colour used was very similar to the recent shade known as National Green and after only a short space of time was not considered to be successful. All the coaches concerned received their more traditional colours at their next repaint. All that is except RF126 which was one of the first examples to be sold and was assumed to have carried this colour to the end. One change resulting from the livery experiment was the decision to incorporate a slightly lighter shade of green for the relief colour. Although this alteration did not affect the original Coach RFs to any extent, all future vehicles intended for Green Line work carried this newer lighter shade.

The introduction of the first of the new Routemaster Coaches intended for Green Line use in 1962 resulted in the first substantial alteration to the make up of the Green Line fleet since 1956. This was hardly surprising as it was always the intention that the RMCs, as they were known, would effect replacement of some of the RF fleet. Broadly speaking, it was intended that the higher capacity of the RMCs would enable a reduction in duplication and the replacement ratio was approximately three RFs for two RMCs. First of the RFs to go was the ex-Private Hire batch 16–25, purloined for Green Line work back in December 1955. The withdrawal of this small batch commenced in August 1962 and although a few were allocated to Central area garages as trainers, all were withdrawn by the year's end. Concurrent with this was the reconversion of RFs 298–313 as buses. It should be recalled that these vehicles were part of the batch converted from buses in 1956 and their interiors had never matched that of the production build. Reconversion to bus also involved conversion to OPO and these were the first ex-Green Line vehicles to be so treated. All were done in August and September 1962 and included the fitting of a new driver's cab door incorporating provision for ticket machine and cash tray, a hinged opening driver's window instead of the normal drop down type and a reversing light. A partial repaint was also effected involving the fleetname panels and relief colour. Internally, bus conversion also involved the reduction of the seating capacity by two by the installation of a small luggage pen directly behind the door on the nearside. This reduced the capacity to 38, but was not undertaken until August 1963. Interior luggage racks were retained as were the mounting brackets to which the route board hooks had been attached. After conversion the majority of the buses concerned were allocated to Chelsham and Amersham Garages to allow replacement of the GS type buses operating therefrom. A point of interest involved RFs 309 and 313 as these had been experimentally painted in a lighter shade of green back in 1960. These two vehicles retained this colour on bus conversion but acquired cream relief and London Transport fleetnames. This hybrid livery was carried until they became due for their next repaint.

The next wind of change blew on the Coach RFs in 1964. Between January 1964 and January 1965 24 examples were deemed surplus to requirements.

Thus it was that RFs 97, 126, 132, 137, 147, 190, 211, 224, 227, 237, 256, 257, 258, 260, 262, 264, 266, 268, 272, 273, 275, 282, 284 and 287 were put on the disposal list. A considerable number of this batch were snapped up by British European Airways who had them fitted with radios and flashing lights and used them for terminal transfer work at Heathrow Airport. The balance were purchased by independents, one of whom, Osbournes of Tollesbury, later became well known as an operator of surplus RFs.

Whilst this was going on a batch of nine vehicles (RFs 34, 66, 89, 99, 101, 110, 138, 175 and 204) were converted to OPO format but retained Coach status. The actual work being undertaken in July. However, at the time no coach routes were one man operated and it was to be a further two years before the status of Green Line was eroded by this economy. Initially, these vehicles were used to cover for shortages of standard Bus RFs around the fleet. Full Green Line livery was retained however.

During 1965 it became increasingly apparent to Green Line Management that the image of Green Line had slipped since the halycon days of the 50s. The RFs by now were almost 15 years old and compared with current offerings were considered to be down market in many people's eyes. Replacement had already been considered and an order for a batch of 14 AEC Reliances had already been placed. Inspection of the RF fleet showed that considering the arduous nature of their duties they were still in remarkable condition and it was thought that a cheaper option might be held by restyling as opposed to replacement. The new Routemaster Coaches had received an enthusiastic response from the travelling public and it was felt that if the RFs could be facelifted to a similar standard they would be good for a few more years service. At the time no one was to realise just how many years that would be!

RF136 was the vehicle chosen to carry the modifications, emerging from Works in March 1966. Suffice to say the restyling was considered successful and a further 174 Coaches were subsequently refurbished. The following chapter deals more extensively with the modernised fleet and readers who wish to know more are referred to that section. What concerns us here is the fate of the remaining 73 unmodernised Green Line RFs.

It had been decided that the balance of Coach RFs not required for Green Line work would be converted to buses. In fact, the alterations were a particularly simple and straightforward operation, coupled with conversion to OPO format at the same time. The same changes which were effected to the RF298–313 batch in 1962 were carried out. In addition the side route board hooks were removed. All of these conversions became 37 seaters at the same time by the removal of the front nearside seat and its replacement by a luggage pen. Bus conversions commenced in September 1965 and by the end of the year 30 vehicles had been so treated. A further eight conversions were undertaken between May and November 1966 and all so far were treated to an overhaul concurrent with the implementations of their reduced status.

Just prior to the commencement of the bus conversions RFs 290–297 inclusive were hired to BEA for use on their new 'Executive Express' service from the West London Air Terminal at Gloucester Road to Heathrow Airport. The period of hire lasted from August 1965 to July 1966 pending delivery to BEA of a batch of new AEC Reliances purpose-built for the service. After the cessation of the BEA hire the coaches concerned were put to store until October 1966 when they entered Works for overhaul and bus conversion. Also included in this consignment was RF289 which had been in store since September 1964. These all became 38 seat vehicles and were the outstanding balance of the 'Bus to Coach' conversions undertaken in 1956. After being reduced to bus status an effort was made to keep the 289–313 batch together in view of the differences between them and other converted vehicles. As a result of this policy at the end of 1966 19 out of the 24 buses could be found allocated to Amersham Garage resulting in this batch being referred to as 'Amersham RFs'. This name stuck long after such buses were transferred to pastures new when overhauling made such dispersals inevitable.

Backtracking slightly to July, from the 10th of that month a new Green Line service was introduced. Numbered 724 the route operated from Romford to High Wycombe and many compared it as a northern version of the 725. Although similar in nature this service kept well away from North London whereas the 725's main bulk operated within what was latterly known as the Greater London Council's area. Nevertheless the 724 introduced the concept of driver only operation to Green Line and was operated by a batch of OPO fitted unmodernised Coach RFs, the only service ever to be so treated. The vehicles used were the batch so converted in July 1964. Soon after introduction it was established that the running time was totally insufficient and an extension in journey time of approximately 30 minutes on a round trip was implemented. This meant that a further vehicle was needed to maintain the service and RF41, only recently converted to a bus, resumed its former coach status. Modernised RFs were allocated as soon as available and this operation of original Coach RFs was extremely shortlived. All of the RFs so employed were subsequently modernised themselves apart from RF41 which reverted to its bus role once again. RF41 proved subsequently to be a 'one off' and its story is told in greater detail later.

The final 26 Coach RFs to be treated to bus conversion were all undertaken between November 1966 and January 1967, but these vehicles were spared the expense of a full overhaul. All Coach RFs remaining after this round of conversions were subsequently facelifted at overhaul, the batch being completed in July 1967. It is thought that the last unmodernised Coach RF to carry Green Line livery was RF63, being the last to be modernised in July 1967. Before we leave the Coach RFs and follow their fortunes in further sections mention must be made of RF41. As with all things London Transport orientated, there is always an anomaly and RF41 fits the bill admirably.

The traditional Central London point for Green Line operations has always been Victoria Eccleston Bridge, and this remains to the present day. RF250 is seen awaiting departure on route 705. Southbound coaches now depart from Buckingham Palace Road following the introduction of an extensive one-way traffic scheme in September 1965. *(DPR Collection)*

RF41 was converted from a coach to a bus in September 1965 receiving an overhaul at the same time. All the normal work was undertaken including the removal of a front nearside seat and its replacement by a luggage pen and to all intents and purposes it was just another conversion. However, in August 1966 RF41 was reconverted to a coach and the seating restored to its original capacity of 39. What isn't known is whether the side board hooks were reinstated but it almost certainly received Green Line livery. The reason for this strange about turn was the fact that another vehicle was needed for new route 724. RF41 was already fitted for driver only operation and was therefore an ideal candidate. As modernised RFs became available so the need for RF41 diminished and in July 1967 it once again was converted to bus status. This time, however, no luggage pen was fitted and the vehicle retained its original interior layout of 39 seats. RF41 remained therefore, internally at least, as a unique vehicles retaining its original coach interior right up until withdrawal in November 1974.

RF137 is carrying a healthy load as it picks up more custom at Potters Bar in March 1953. In those days the Green Line network was highly regarded by the travelling public and the respect in which coach crews were held was high. RF137 was one of the first of its class to be sold, departing for pastures new in October 1964. *(Geoff Rixon)*

Routes 723/A were not to have the benefits of RF operation for very long as further RFs were needed for expansion. It was decided, from July 1954, to convert these routes to RT operation so releasing a total of 24 RFs for use elsewhere. RF106 is seen on route 723 some two years prior to the change. *(Alan Cross)*

RF281 passes Bushy Park, Hampton Court on 1st July 1953, the first day of operation of the new South Orbital route 725. Despite this being the first day a capacity load appears to be carried. Where's all the traffic gone though? *(Geoff Rixon)*

Even in 1953 the practice of putting new coaches on to bus work was prevalent. RF85 lays over at New Barnet Station prior to undertaking a rural trip to Broxbourne. *(Geoff Rixon)*

Above: **The standard Green Line RF interior.** *(London Transport Museum)*

Facing page top: **Some Bus RFs were converted to Coaches in 1956. One such example was RF300 seen here on bus work at Dorking North Station. A different method of fixing the route sideboards was employed on these conversions and as can be clearly seen the vehicle retains bus style seating.** *(DPR Collection)*

Facing page middle: **RF282 is seen at Dartford Garage whilst working on route 423B. In later years the 423B was significant in being operated by coaches prior to coach service. At the time of this view, suspected to be in 1954, this coach was allocated to Northfleet Garage so one assumes that various interworkings between routes were rife. It can be safely assumed that this vehicle was undertaking bus duties at the time. It was absolute sacrilege for a coach to go out on Green Line without sideboards during this period.** *(DPR Collection)*

Facing page bottom: **Some Coach RFs were allocated to bus work from 1959 onwards to release OPO fitted Bus RFs for use elsewhere. The routes concerned were considered to justify crew operation and the use of OPO format buses on these routes was considered wasteful. One of the services to receive Coach RFs was the 391 from St Albans Garage. RF295 is illustrated at St Albans Garage forecourt. This was one of the early bus to coach conversions undertaken in 1956.** *(Alan Cross)*

425 WESTCOTT AND DORKING NTH STN
GREEN LINE
NLE 519

423a DARTFORD AND LITTLEBROOK
GREEN LINE
RF282
MLL 819

MILE HOUSE ESTATE
391 CITY STATION St PETERS STREET
RF295
GREEN LINE
NLE 514

This page top: **Soon after the RFs were introduced a new style of destination blind appeared. Coloured black and amber, this style remained up until the mid-1960s. During this period of time very little changes were effected to the Green Line network and even less to the vehicles themselves. RF56 is seen at Denham on route 711 with only about 40 minutes of its cross London journey left ahead of it.** *(DPR Collection)*

This page bottom: **RF157 heads south through Harpenden in August 1965. Slip board brackets can just be discerned below the nearside windscreen, the purpose of which in this period of time is unknown.** *(Gerald Mead)*

Facing page top: **Aldgate Bus Station provides the location for RF49 on route 720. Standards have obviously slipped since the 1950s. In those days it would be unheard of for a coach to run in service carrying the accident damage that can be seen on the offside at the front of this vehicle.** *(Peter J. Relf)*

Facing page middle: **Tunbridge Wells was the southern extremity of route 704 which was the first route of all to operate RF coaches. The garage at Tunbridge Wells was unique within London Transport as it purely operated Green Line coaches, no bus work ever being scheduled. The town also boasted a 'Green Line Coach Station' where RF180 is seen after a rather heavy shower! Some years later the small garage at Tunbridge Wells was closed, all work being transferred to the premises at Dunton Green.** *(Author's Collection)*

Facing page bottom: **A brave attempt to encourage travel by Green Line was new route 727, the introduction of which from November 1964 operated via the newly opened M1 Motorway. Soon after introduction the motorway was closed for repairs (nothing ever changes, does it) and the service diverted accordingly. Not surprising was the fact that the crew regularly outnumbered the passengers and soon after the route was withdrawn.** *(Alan Cross)*

720 BISHOPS STORTFORD
LONDON BISHOPS STORTFORD OR HARLOW
GREEN LINE
RF 49
LYF 400

704 WINDSOR
704
GREEN LINE
RF 180
MLL 567

727 EXPRESS TRING
LONDON
727 EXPRESS TRING
GREEN LINE
RF 52
LYF 380

August 1960 saw 16 Green Line RFs outshopped in a much lighter green than hitherto. These coaches were allocated to Reigate and High Wycombe Garages for use on route 711. Needless to say the livery did not impress and all received more traditional colours at their next repaint. All that is except RF126 which was sold without being repainted. Seen here is RF271 on Reigate Garage forecourt.
(Gerald Mead)

A most unusual working was that of two of the light green Coach RFs on Central area route 206. RFs 33 and 42 were the coaches concerned, being allocated to Fulwell Garage from February–May 1963. Other than the use of RF107 in February 1963 from Leyton Garage this was the only known example of Coach RFs operating on Central routes. Seen here is RF33 on stand at Hampton Court Station.
(Gerald Mead)

Concurrent with the modernisation of selected Green Line RFs (see page 61) was the introduction of another style of blind. This was black and yellow and this style of design remained until very late in London Country days. It was not the intention that this newer blind should be used other than in refurbished coaches but as can be imagined if it fitted, use it! RF202 in Buckingham Palace Road in May 1966 had only five months to go before modernisation and carries the new blind. This coach has subsequently been preserved by London Country South East, latterly named the Kentish Bus and Coach Co. *(Gerald Mead)*

A quiet Sunday in Aylesbury finds RF170 on route 707. Here again the new style blind is fitted. Oxted Holland was, in fact, a little further on than the more normal weekday terminus at Oxted Station and was an effective way of covering a small section of a local bus route that didn't run on Sundays. *(J. G. S. Smith)*

CRAWLEY
405
London Redhill
Gatwick Airport
LONDON TRANSPORT
PAY AS YOU ENTER
PLEASE
LYF 443

341
St ALBANS
LONDON TRANSPORT
RF 86
PAY AS YOU ENTER
PLEASE
LYF 437

GUILDFORD
432
MLL 604

Facing page top: **Following the introduction of new Routemaster Coaches in 1962 and service reductions throughout the 1960s, a programme of converting Coach RFs to OPO buses was carried out from September 1965 onwards. Externally the vehicles received all the standard fittings associated with OPO conversion (opening cab window, reversing light, etc.) and a repaint into bus livery. Externally at least the vehicles were identical to the standard Bus RFs and it was only upon boarding that the previous status of the vehicles was apparent. RF92 stands at the old West Croydon Bus Station on route 405. This service was originally OPO on Sundays only, an economy which manifested itself in the Country area from 1968 onwards.** *(Peter J. Relf)*

Facing page middle: **Another Sunday only OPO conversion was the 341 which was RF operated from Hertford Garage but MB operated from Hatfield. RF86 is seen in Hertford Car Park representing the Hertford allocation on this route in June 1969.** *(J. G. S. Smith)*

Facing page bottom: **The converted Bus Coach RFs were scattered far and wide and were completely integrated with the standard bus examples. RF217 is seen here on route 432.** *(DPR Collection)*

This page top: **The first coaches to buses conversion was undertaken in 1962 and involved some of the batch that had originally been converted *from* buses back in 1956. Most were used to replace GS types at Chesham and Amersham Garages and shown here is RF306 in Chesham Broadway. Unlike future conversions, this type of vehicle retained mounting brackets for roof sideboards and were thus easily distinguishable. In years to come the majority of this batch migrated to Amersham Garage in an attempt to keep their non-standard features under one roof. As a result they soon acquired the nickname of 'Amersham RFs' which stuck for the remainder of their lives.** *(Gerald Mead)*

This page bottom: **Some of the 1956 batch of coach conversions were hired to BEA in August 1965 for use on their new 'Executive Express' service. After return from BEA the vehicles were all stored and then subsequently converted to buses. RF296, carrying BEA insignia, is seen at Aldenham Works in October 1966 prior to overhaul and bus conversion.** *(Alan Cross)*

THE CENTRAL BUS RFs

RF289–513: *Original Build.*

RF289–294: *Converted to Green Line coaches in March 1956.*

RF295–313: *Renumbered RF514-532 in March 1956.*

RF533–538: *Transferred to Central fleet in December 1956,*
retained Country Bus livery until January 1958.

The first of the batch of Central RFs were taken into stock in August 1952, the first three, RFs 289–291, entering service the following month at Muswell Hill Garage on route 210. The most noticeable difference to the Green Line and Private Hire RFs delivered earlier was the lack of platform doors whilst situated over the entrance was a small 'roofbox' which carried a plate bearing the route number upon which the bus was operating. This latter feature was unique to the red RFs. Internally, 41 seats were carried, two more above that of the Coach RFs and at the front these were arranged in 'bench fashion' as opposed to the more usual 'two and two' layout. No luggage racks or saloon heaters were fitted. The lack of doors was entirely due to the insistence of the Metropolitan Police who were the licensing authority at the time. No such objection existed over doored Coach RFs operating through the Metropolitan area however! Livery was standard bus red with cream relief and black wheel mudguards.

Deliveries were extremely rapid and by the year's end 89 vehicles had arrived. During this time RF330 was displayed at the MCCW stand at the 1952 Commercial Motor Show at Earls Court. By March 1953 all 225 vehicles had been received into stock and garages at Bromley, Croydon, Dalston, Hounslow, Merton, Muswell Hill, New Cross, Norbiton, Sidcup, Sutton and West Green had been the lucky recipients. Omitted from this list was Kingston which in later years was best remembered for the fact that it was in possession of a 100% RF allocation; Kingston's first RFs not being allocated until July 1959.

The higher capacity of the RFs over the vehicles that had been replaced led to a general thinning of the level of service provided in many cases. As a result, from October 1953 sufficient spare RFs had been gathered to enable an allocation to be made at Loughton Garage on route 254.

In February 1956 various changes were made to the make up of the Central area RF fleet. Although of a minor nature compared to the upheaval of the Green Line and Country Bus fleets a certain amount of renumbering within the class took place. Firstly, RFs 289–294 were converted to Green Line coaches. Initially, this only involved the fitting of platform doors and a repaint into the appropriate livery. At first overhaul the installation of luggage racks, heaters and flooring took place. To all intents these vehicles were now part of the Green Line fleet and their subsequent history will be found within that section. RFs 295–313 were renumbered 514–532. This was done so as to keep the different types of RF in numbered batches. The missing 295–313 also became Green Line coaches but these were converted from Country Bus RFs.

The transfer of RFs 289–294 to the Green Line fleet brought to a head a disagreement between Trade Union and Management over the use of surplus red RFs. An agreement had been made some time previous that such spare RFs would be used to effect replacement of manual transmission single deckers within the Central fleet. As far as the Trade Union was concerned this was a direct contravention of that agreement and some forthright representations were made. Eventually Management conceded and as a result six Country Bus RFs (533–538) were transferred to Central stock, being allocated to Sidcup Garage.

To cover a temporary shortage of red RFs, the operations at Sidcup Garage had been maintained since October 1956 by a number of green Bus RFs. With the transfer of these six examples Sidcup now boasted an allocation of 16 green RFs. Apart from the allocation of a further green example in October 1957 the situation remained until January 1958 when all the green RFs other than 533–538 were transferred back to the Country area. At this time these six examples finally received red livery and had their platform doors removed. So ended the saga of the RFs that had commenced with the intention in early 1956 to bolster the Green Line fleet.

The operation of these green RFs in the Central area threw up a particularly interesting anomaly, namely the fitment of platform doors. As mentioned previously, the Metropolitan Police did not permit doored operation and in the past when doored Country area vehicles had been borrowed (such as the 15T13s at Norbiton in 1956) the offending doors had been bolted in the open position. It is reasonable to assume that similar treatment was afforded to the Sidcup RFs. The same query re-occurs later in 1959 when the first Central vehicles had doors fitted as a result of conversion to OPO format.

The operation of RFs as OPO vehicles had been found to be totally satisfactory in the Country area and thoughts now turned to attempt to introduce a similar system on the Metropolis. Attempt being the word as the Trade Union was totally opposed to this form of operation. Nevertheless the batch of vehicles from RFs 502–538 were converted from April 1959 to permit driver only operation. Modifications involved installing a hinged cab window in lieu of the drop down type previously fitted. Seating capacity was reduced by two as a result of fitting a small luggage pen immediately inside the entrance and a reversing light and platform doors were installed. Astute readers will realise that 533–538 only had their doors removed in January 1958 and yet just over a year later the reverse process was now being applied!

However, as was expected, the introduction of Central area OPO fell foul of the Trade Union who successfully resisted its introduction for a further five and a half years! In the meantime no further vehicles were modified and although some OPO fitted RFs did operate as crew vehicles for a few days in May 1959, the majority were put to store at, of all places, Grays Country Area Garage. Most of the stored vehicles were relicensed in June and were allocated to Norbiton and Uxbridge Garages where they were used to effect replacement of TD type vehicles. It appears that this batch of RFs were placed into service with their newly acquired doors bolted in the open position so as not to contravene police regulations. One presumes that no objection to doored OPO vehicles existed!

Meanwhile a use was found for five of the OPO fitted buses when, in July, RFs 509, 532, 534, 535 and 538 were allocated to Reigate Country Area Garage and used as driver only vehicles on routes 440/A. Ironically, therefore, the first use of red RFs in OPO mode was in the Country area. Even more ironic was the fact that until January 1958 three of the vehicles concerned had been green anyway! These buses returned to the Central area fold in 1960 as the overhaul programme was causing a short term shortage of red RFs. To assist in covering the programme a number of green RFs were also loaned, being allocated to Kingston Garage until the demand on the Central fleet ceased. Such loans of 'wrong liveried' vehicles were fairly common throughout the late 50s and 60s. (See Appendix G.) One point, did Kingston's green vehicle allocation have their doors bolted open?

Other than the heater fitting programme (to OPO format vehicles) the Central fleet enjoyed a period of relative stability until 18th November 1964; the only other point of interest being the withdrawal of RF464 through fire damage, the first RF to be removed from stock. However, agreement had at last been reached for the extension of OPO into the Central area and 18th November was the date set for the conversions to take place. Four routes, the 201 from Norbiton, 206 from Fulwell, 216 from Kingston and 250 from Romford North Street, were all converted to driver only operation. The first Central area services to be so worked for 15 years. As soon as it was realised by Management that it was 'all systems go' as far as OPO was concerned, a rolling programme of converting RFs to OPO format was undertaken. From January 1965 to September 1966 a further 110 red RFs were treated, leaving a total of 77 vehicles in original condition.

Although the Green Line fleet had been heater fitted since construction, the ordinary vehicles making up the bus fleets in common with other vehicle types had had to do without. Following a change of policy in the early 60s it was decided that heaters would be fitted to any vehicle where its expected life would be over eight years. Resulting from this the first of the red RFs were so fitted at the beginning of 1964. The eight year ruling was strictly applied and this effectively excluded any RF that was to remain as a crew vehicle. All OPO buses eventually received the luxury of heaters but their crew operated brothers were, it could be said, left out in the cold!

Another policy decision which affected the RFs was taken in 1965 when grey replaced cream as the relief colour. First to be treated were RFs 449, 508 and 509.

During January 1969 the Central area received an influx of 13 green Country area OPO fitted RFs. Originally 25 such vehicles were to be transferred but in the event no more were to follow. It was intended to extend OPO operation and was considered a cheaper option to use surplus green RFs as opposed to convert further crew examples to OPO. The vehicles concerned, RFs 545, 563, 570, 580, 590, 598, 602, 603, 608, 617, 627, 632 and 685, were all allocated to Muswell Hill Garage and initially operated as crew buses on route 210 in full Country colours. Repaints were effected in June 1969 and the vehicles remained crew operated until 24th January 1970 when the 210 was converted to OPO using this same batch of buses.

Even at this late stage LT still considered the RF a useful vehicle to allow more conversions to OPO. Backtracking slightly to March 1969, routes 80/A at Sutton Garage were so treated whilst from 16th January 1971 a large scheme at Uxbridge saw 30 such vehicles allocated. Whereas the Sutton buses were scraped up from around the fleet and were all OPO conversions from the 1965/66 programme, those at Uxbridge were a further batch of crew buses modified for OPO in 1970. Most of the vehicles were from Bromley Garage where a rolling programme had been undertaken since the previous November to enable sufficient OPO vehicles to be available at Uxbridge from 16th January. A float was created and as the vehicles were converted they returned to Bromley and operated as crew buses until needed at Uxbridge.

A standard Bus RF interior. Both Central and Country area vehicles were identical apart from the provision of platform doors on Country examples. As detailed in the text, Central buses received doors on conversion to OPO format. *(London Transport Museum)*

These conversions differed from those previous by having a more modern style of door utilising two panes of glass rather than four. The luggage pen was of a different design to previous conversions as was the cab door and cash tray arrangement. One exception was RF390 which, although modernised, utilised the parts from RF590 which having been involved in a serious accident was withdrawn. All of these conversions were heater fitted even though the majority never achieved the eight year life that had previously been considered a necessity. This batch of RFs became known as 'Uxbridge RFs' and, in later years when such vehicles were transferred elsewhere, the name stuck. It should be noted, however, that the majority were withdrawn rather than transferred and in later years the RFs at Uxbridge were just as any other. One vehicle, RF346, managed to be recertified as one of the last of the class to see service at Kingston Garage. In this role it was the one surviving Uxbridge RF but a serious accident at Esher one morning prematurely terminated its service career. Fortunately, its driver was unhurt.

1971 saw the last operation of crew operated RFs. Over the preceding years their replacement had either been by new AEC Swifts or, as documented earlier, by substituting OPO fitted RFs in their place (as OPO buses). As 1971 dawned only two routes remained which were crew RF operated, namely the 227 from Bromley Garage which, as mentioned above, received AEC Swifts from 2nd January, and the 236 operated by Dalston and Leyton Garages. This service succumbed to Swift operation from 17th April, the last crew operated single deckers in London running in for the last time the previous night. In fact, the night of 16th April can be associated with two other London lasts. In the same area as the 236 and indeed operated from Dalston Garage as well, the same night yielded the last lowbridge buses in the metropolis, the RLH type, whilst a far more subtle last, common to both of these vehicle types, was the fact that from the following day no buses remained in passenger service carrying cream as the relief colour. This livery common since before the Second World War was consigned to the archives.

Progressing to 1974 thoughts had now turned towards replacement of the remaining RFs in stock. It was decided that a certain proportion could be replaced by Swifts whilst on routes where physical restrictions prevented the operation of these larger buses, a new smaller type of vehicle would have to be obtained. It was subsequently decided upon the Bristol LH as replacement and this in itself caused one of the most unusual workings for many a time. LT approached the NBC subsidiary, London Country (whose formation and affect on the RF class is told elsewhere within this book), who had recently taken delivery of some LHs, to see if such a vehicle could be borrowed for evaluation purposes. At the time London Country were suffering from chronic vehicle shortage and the only way an LH could be spared was if during the time of the loan it could be replaced with another vehicle. So it was that RF370 was loaned to Amersham Garage (from whence the LH had originated) during July 1974 and saw service on the vast majority of Amersham routes. Whereas in the past the loan of vehicles between Central and Country department (see Appendix G) had been fairly common, this was the first time since 1971 that a red RF had worked in the Country area. One further instance of such a working did occur in August 1974 when RF426, a Kingston allocated bus, replaced a failed AEC Reliance on Green Line 727 and worked through to St Albans where it was further substituted. This is generally thought to have been the last time such a working occurred. The upshot of all this was the placing of an order in November 1974 for a batch of 95 Bristol LHs which were subsequently classified BL. The first seeds of Central RF replacement had been sown.

At the time most of the remaining RF routes were what was termed as 'Out County', that is services that operated outside the former Greater London Council area, all of which received a subsidy from the local county councils in whose areas the routes served. When the order for LHs was placed, a general 'belt tightening' exercise was in force which led to a number of service reductions or even withdrawals, thanks to reductions in county council financial support. In February 1976 the first BLs were taken into stock and, not surprisingly in view of attitudes at the time, the services for which they were originally destined had changed considerably. A number of these vehicles were surplus to requirements even before they were delivered! In order to utilise these spare vehicles a number were allocated to RF routes where the initial form of replacement was intended to be AEC Swifts. Even so, as more service reductions took place so more spare vehicles were thrown up and only a few years later the first members of the class were put up for disposal. The BLs also had an alarming tendency to catch fire, and whilst not the intended method was a very timely way of reducing the stock of surplus vehicles!

At this stage it was intended that the last Central RFs would be those allocated to Uxbridge on route 223, but following a change of plan the venue changed to Hounslow and routes 202 and 237. However, it was then discovered that the pits at Kingston Garage were unsuitable for the AEC Swifts which were the intended replacement vehicles for the RFs on routes 218 and 219. As a short term solution it was decided to recertify a batch of 25 RFs until the problem could be solved. Most of the recertification work was carried out at Hanwell and Stonebridge Park Garages. All were repainted and appeared in many differing styles of livery. For example, some remained with traditional gold fleetnames and numbers whilst others received the filled bullseye symbol which previously had been associated with more modern vehicle types. Amongst those recertified were RFs 314 and 471 which had previously been employed on staff bus duties outstationed at Reigate LCBS Garage. In this role both had been 'customised' with twin fog lights and later styles of fleetnames (see photographs on page 49). RF314 was unique in retaining twin foglights after recertification for passenger service. Also included in the batch was RF346, the last remaining 'Uxbridge RF' mentioned earlier.

One change which brought to a close an era started in 1964 was the replacement of the Ultimate ticket machines with Almex E Electric Machines thought to be in early 1978. RFs and Ultimate had gone hand in hand and indeed these were the last of this type of machine to be used in London. An interesting repercussion resulting from this was that the RFs at Kingston were no longer route bound to the 218 and 219, as Almex machines were now used on all of Kingston Garage's OPO services. Resulting from this RFs once again began to make appearances on routes 71 (a one off at the request of enthusiasts), 215 (very rare, only one or two appearances) and 216 (an almost daily occurrence). Concurrently, the occasional BL was to be found on route 218 or 219.

Although most of the RFs that were recertified received four year tickets, replacement came sooner than expected. Surrey County Council as the paymasters requested that economies be made throughout the county. An examination of routes 218 and 219 showed that the only way to achieve any form of worthwhile saving would be by reducing the headway and substituting larger vehicles and this is precisely what happened. The old problem which had spared the RFs in the first place re-occurred, only this time was easily solved by reallocating the two services to the neighbouring Norbiton Garage. To replace the 218/9 allocation Kingston received part of Norbiton's crew route 65. The date set for the last day of RF operation was 30th March 1979. Leading up to this time much continued as before. Route 216 more often than not also had a small number of RFs allocated to it at the expense of the 218/9 which made do with a couple of BLs. During the last week of RF operation RF507 was chosen as the bus that would perform the last rites on the forthcoming Friday night, primarily as little work would have to be done to it to restore it to early 1960's livery as was the intention. The vehicle was generally spruced up and the cream window surrounds reinstated, whilst for the last day of all a liberal amount of Christmas decorations filled the interior. RF507 duly performed the final journey, duplicated by RFs 314 and 492 to cater for the crowds. In addition a number of preserved RFs were present, the whole ensemble arriving to a crowd of hundreds at Kingston Garage in the early hours of Saturday 31st March. Later the same morning RFs 510, 511 and 512 were used for a farewell enthusiaists' tour covering the whole of routes 218 and 219 whilst RF507 took part on a staff private hire.

RF operation in the Central area had spanned almost 27 years, a remarkable tribute to a remarkable bus.

The first Central area route to receive RFs was the 210. RF430 is seen at Hampstead Heath carrying a particularly heavy load typical of this service at the time. *(Author's Collection)*

East London had many busy single deck services where physical restrictions precluded the use of double deck vehicles. One such example was route 208A and RF448 is seen at Maryland Station along with its crew. Note the Bell Punch ticket machine. *(Geoff Rixon)*

As physical restrictions were overcome many RF routes were consequently upgraded to double deck status. Route 233 was particularly interesting in so much as it was partially double decked in September 1955. These being short workings between Finsbury Park and Alexander Park. Full double deck conversion came from March 1959. RF458 lays over at Finsbury Park soon after introduction in 1953. The bus carries an earlier style of blind more readily associated with pre-war vehicles. The West Green Garage plates would be a collector's item nowadays. *(Geoff Rixon)*

Brand new RF383 stands outside the old Norbiton Garage. A small number of Central RFs were experimentally fitted with semaphore indicators as can be clearly seen here. In true LT fashion *all* RFs had the provision for this facility (note the 'plates' in other photographs) but very few were actually equipped. It was subsequently decided that semaphores were not a practical proposition, the one on the nearside for instance was directly in line with waiting passengers!, and it was to be some years hence before front indicators again appeared, this time in the more familiar 'dogs-ear' format which has survived on Routemasters to the present day. *(Geoff Rixon)*

RF366 loads at the old Hounslow Garage before departing for Chertsey. Today's 237 route operates as far as Sunbury but, as compensation, was back-projected to Shepherds Bush in 1976. As a result of these changes Routemasters were latterly seen on this service. *(Geoff Rixon)*

Sidcup Garage was the first in London to lose its RF allocation when both its routes, the 228 and 241 received RTs in November 1958. At one time the RF allocation at Sidcup was almost 100% made up of green liveried examples. In 1953 RF507 could be found at Sidcup and is seen here on route 241. In years to come RF507 found itself as the last example to run in passenger service with London Transport (see back cover) but by then the bus had carried four different bodies. *(Author's Collection)*

Route 234A, operated by Croydon Garage, received RFs in January 1953 and remained RF operated until January 1977, a remarkable achievement, which could never be matched by present day buses! RF412 loads at Wallington. *(Alan Cross)*

Route 208 remained RF operated for many years, being one of the last services to be worked with crew operated examples. RF310 illustrated here was subsequently renumbered to RF529 to make way for a further batch of Green Line format vehicles. *(Alan Cross)*

Another RF that was to carry a much higher fleetnumber was RF298, subsequently renumbered to RF517. Route 213 became double deck operated following the rebuilding of Worcester Park Station Bridge in 1963. At one time, it was intended that this route would be operated by RLHs but bridge rebuilding came sooner. *(Alan Cross)*

Wimbledon Station stand was situated outside the Police Station and in later years at least was a popular location with bus crews, being out of the public gaze! The crew of RF339 enjoy the peace and tranquillity before embarking on yet another short trip to Raynes Park. *(Alan Cross)*

As RF routes were upgraded to double deck operation so a number of further routes received the displaced RFs replacing the older T or TD type vehicles. Route 211 was one such example receiving a batch of RFs so displaced from Sidcup Garage. In time the 211 was also double decked and survived to be incorporated in the Ealing Flat Fare scheme implemented in the late 1960s. RF324 waits for departure at the Greenford Red Lion stand, still recognisable today. *(Peter J. Relf)*

September 1959 in West Drayton sees RF349 heading for Laleham on route 224. From 8th May 1963 this service was converted to RT operation but history has a knack of repeating itself. From 16th January 1971 RFs returned to the 224 albeit this time driver only operated. As far as is known this and the 224B were the only routes where this happened in the Central area. *(Gerald Mead)*

Over the years routes 210 and 236 have had a particularly confusing history. Originally the 210 operated from Finsbury Park to Golders Green and the 236 from Leytonstone to Golders Green with a peak hour projection to Stroud Green. On Sundays the 236 operated through to Golders Green over the 210 route but at one time the reverse situation applied and the 210 ran through to Leytonstone. The terminals of both these services were changed many times over the years and for one short space of time in 1970 OPO RFs ran alongside crew RFs over the same section of road. Seen here is Leyton Garage's RF403, photographed during the time that the 210 operated through to Leytonstone. The date of the photograph being September 1965. *(Gerald Mead)*

A sunny August day in Finsbury Park in 1967 shows RF357 on route 236. This service was the last to be operated with crew RFs retaining them as late as April 1971. OPO format RFs were to last eight year longer. *(Gerald Mead)*

Although a batch of red RFs were converted to OPO format in 1959 it was to be November 1964 before Trade Union agreement could be reached for their operation as driver only vehicles. In the meantime they were used as normal crew buses but with the doors bolted in the open position so as to keep in line with police regulations at the time. RF503 stands at Hampton Court Station on route 201, showing its new-acquired non-operable doors. *(Gerald Mead)*

In November 1964 route 216, operated by Kingston Garage, became OPO and as a result OPO RFs now appeared on crew routes with operating doors! Allocation of the right sort of RF to their respective routes, initially at least must have caused a great deal of patience, made easier as time went on by the allocation of further OPO fitted vehicles. Here we see RF505 on route 215 in March 1965. Routes 215/A were eventually converted to OPO in January 1966. *(Gerald Mead)*

The LT official photo of a newly-converted Central area OPO RF. The 'roofbox' number can be clearly seen although this feature was not to last long once OPO was introduced. Another feature, unique to Central RFs was the placing of roof advertisements. That illustrated here sensibly advertises 'Red Rovers' but a considerable number of RFs in Central service for some strange reason carried posters proclaiming the Country area version – the Green Rover (see page 39). *(London Transport Museum)*

Route 250 was an early conversion to driver only operation and RF440 is seen at Abridge crossing the River Roding. *(J. G. S. Smith)*

Route 20B was introduced from October 1965 so as to effect an economy over the northern section of route 20 between Loughton and Epping. Apart from being the lowest service number ever to be displayed upon an RF this route was somewhat unusual in being RF OPO on Sundays–Fridays but double deck crew operated on Saturdays! The OPO conversion of route 20 in June 1969 brought about the withdrawal of the 20B and the reinstatement of route 20 to its original terminus. RF445 is seen at Epping. *(J. G. S. Smith)*

The introduction of driver only operation allowed the introduction of some new services hitherto prevented by the initial high crewing costs. One such example was route 136, introduced from 8th August 1966 which provided the first ever service over Harrow-on-the-Hill. This service subsequently survived and is still maintained today albeit in a different form. RF421, minus its 'paye' slipboard is seen in Roxeth Hill, Harrow. Quite what the driver of the Hillman Minx is trying to achieve is debatable! *(J. G. S. Smith)*

Route 291 was introduced as a localisation of route 129 in October 1965 and introduced the RF class to Barking Garage. RF384 is seen at Ilford. *(Gerald Mead)*

(OCT 1965 – MAR. 1973)

41

Route 211 (the Hounslow version) was a short lived attempt to localise the southern end of route 111. Operation was by OPO RF on Mondays–Fridays but on Saturdays was RT operated and extended on from Hampton to Kingston. Today route 111 operates throughout as a driver only service and the 211 is a thing of the past. Carrying the later style of 'paye' slipboard is RF360, seen in Hanworth.
(J. G. S. Smith)

RFs abound at Hounslow Bus Station. The driver of RF442 pauses for a chat prior to a journey to Chertsey, whilst in an adjacent bay an unidentified example prepares to set off for Richmond on route 202. Red buses to Chertsey are now a thing of the past and the RFs themselves are long since gone.
(DPR Collection)

One experimental service that was doomed to a short existence was the 151. One RF provided a shuttle between Sutton and Belmont during off peak periods and this view of RF382 illustrates to perfection the justification for an early withdrawal! Introduced from 10th October 1970 the route existed little over six months before cessation. *(Gerald Mead)*

Sutton Garage, having lost their original RFs in 1963 when route 213 was double-decked, received a further allocation in March 1969 when routes 80 and 80A were rerouted and converted to OPO. RF485 is seen outside Sutton Garage on route 80 a few months before Bristol LHs removed RFs from Sutton Garage for the second and final time. *(Steve Fennell)*

Old Lodge Lane, Purley was the southern terminus of route 234A which is the location for this view of RF392. Originally destined to have its RFs replaced by SMS type buses, it eventually received BLs as the rear overhang of an SMS caused a problem when undertaking the turning manoeuvre at this point. *(John Parkin)*

The Uxbridge OPO scheme of January 1971 required a further batch of crew RFs to be modified to OPO format. It had been many years since such conversions had been undertaken and not surprisingly the style of alteration was different to what had gone before. Internally the cab door and cash tray was of a restyled pattern whilst perhaps the most noticeable alteration was the fitting of new style doors with only one pane of glass per door instead of two. RF345 seen here at Hayes shows the different type of door clearly. *(Colin Stannard)*

Route 224B was part of the above mentioned scheme, receiving RFs in place of RTs. Latterly buses on this route carried a unique style of blind shown by RF364 at West Drayton. *(Steve Fennell)*

RFs 350 and 431 pace each other around the then new Staines Gyratory system in March 1976. Route 224 only had a further two months existence in this part of Surrey before spending cuts prompted its demise. *(Steve Fennell)*

Staines West Station stand was a favourite location to photograph RFs and a Saturday visit always produced a suitable quantity of vehicles upon which to point the camera. Such was the case here with, from left to right, RFs 472, 459 and 521 all taking their stands. *(Steve Fennell)*

Also seen at Staines West is RF463 about to leave on route 216. *(Steve Fennell)*

Some crew double deck services were converted to driver only operation on Sundays when passenger usage was low and OPO could be justified. RF522 is seen at Kingston on one such example, the 71. The Leatherhead service eventually became a daily OPO operation but not before the RFs were withdrawn. Today route 71 operates as far south as Chessington Zoo, the Leatherhead section being a casualty of reduced county council support. *(G. Mead)*

Whereas in the Country area the use of RFs as substitutions for other vehicles was particularly common, in the Central area such instances could be counted on the fingers of one hand. Seen here is RF384 operating on route 270. This was as a direct result of SM shortage and was based on local initiative. However, operation was extremely short lived due to Trade Union intervention. *(DPR Collection)*

During 1969 a batch of 13 green RFs were transferred to Central area stock and allocated to Muswell Hill Garage for use on route 210. (See page 60.) They were subsequently repainted red, and following SMS conversion of the 210 were dispersed far and wide. On overhaul some of the green bodies became dispersed and ended up on normal red stock numbers. These were always distinguishable from genuine red bodies as no provision had ever been made for the roof number box on green RFs and as a result the telltale roofbox rivets which all red bodies carried were not there! After the last overhaul cycle these bodies ended up on RFs 352, 421, 428, 452, 489, 495 and 502, and some of these survived until the last day of red RF operation in March 1979. Some of these ex-green RFs never received an overhaul and therefore retained their genuine 'green bodies'. Conversely, RFs 545, 590, 598, 602, 603, 627, 632 and 685 received bodies which were of red pedigree and the site of the roofbox could be clearly seen!

Seen above is RF627 at Theydon Bois on route 250. The bus is now carrying a 'red body' which it received on overhaul in February 1972. Route 250 was also the first RF route to receive blinds where the route number was on the nearside, whilst below is seen RF563 at Kingston on route 219. On overhaul in November 1972 this bus received the body from RF685 and is therefore a genuine ex-green RF. *(Both Steve Fennell)*

Route 251 lost its RFs in January 1977. As with the 234A, SMSs were the intended replacement but in the event BLs were used instead. RF510 is illustrated at Mill Hill one week before RFs were removed from this part of London for ever. This particular vehicle survived as one of the last batch to see service at Kingston in March 1979. *(Steve Fennell)*

The final RFs were all recertified and appeared in many different styles of livery. Some were outshopped in traditional manner with gold fleetnames, etc., whilst others, like RF437 illustrated here, received the more modern bullseye symbol. Wood Street, Kingston is the location of this view. *(Paul Hulyer)*

Some surplus RFs were used to replace the last examples of the GS vehicles on staff bus duties to and from Chiswick Works. Two such vehicles were outstationed at Reigate London Country Garage and most weekends could be found on the forecourt of that establishment. Both the vehicles concerned had been customised with twin foglamps as well as receiving various livery alterations. Seen on Reigate forecourt are RFs 314 and 471, RF471 being the first example ever to carry the filled in bullseye transfer on its side. Both of these vehicles were subsequently returned to PSV service and finished their days at Kingston Garage as some of the last examples to see such service. Interestingly RF314 retained its twin foglamps but RF471 reverted to its original style when PSV service was resumed. RF314 for the last few years of its life ran as a unique vehicle – Green Line RF179 looks on.
(Steve Fennell)

Even when on staff bus duties RF314 was unique. It being the only RF ever to carry the lined bullseye as its fleetname. The bullseye is clearly visible in this view of RF314 descending Blackborough Road, Reigate.
(Steve Fennell)

'Red on Green'

From time to time, depending upon the demands of the overhaul programme short term shortages of RFs occurred. In such cases red RFs could operate on Country services and vice versa. Whereas the use of red RFs in the Country area was fairly if not regularly common the reverse was very much a different proposition. RF498 is seen at Batford operating from St Albans Garage on route 355. *(Gerald Mead)*

When route 336 was converted to driver only operation in October 1965 it coincided with the Country RF overhaul programme and consequently standard green RFs were in short supply. As a result the initial conversion was undertaken by red RFs and RF368 is seen at Watford Junction. Red RF operation on this particular service only lasted a matter of weeks before sufficient green vehicles were available. *(Alan Cross)*

A most unusual operation was the use of a red RF on route 705. The bus was undoubtedly an emergency substitute for a defective Green Line example and is seen in Victoria Garage. A minimum fare slipboard for route 237 is carried which is fairly conclusive that this was a Hounslow allocated RF. RF524 was only allocated to Hounslow between January and May 1965 which effectively dates this view. *(Author's Collection)*

After the infamous split of 1970 examples of red RFs working in the Country area understandably became somewhat rare. However, as a temporary measure five crew RFs were loaned to London Country, four of which remained until February 1971. RF374 is seen at Dorking Garage on route 449. *(Ken Harris)*

RF388 operated from both East Grinstead and Crawley Garages duting its period of loan. Such was the enthusiasm of EG's staff that the bus inadvertently received London Country legal lettering and fleetname which, once the mistake was noticed, was hastily rectified! RF388, with conductor clearly in view, is seen at East Grinstead on route 428. *(Ken Harris)*

THE COUNTRY BUS RFs

RF514–700: *Original Build.*

RF514–516: *Converted to Green Line coaches in March 1956 and renumbered*
RF518–532 *RF295-RF297 and RF299-RF313 respectively.*

Prototype OPO conversions.

RF517: *RF517 renumbered RF697 in March 1956.*

RF647: *RF647 renumbered RF698 in January 1956 (and vice versa).*

RF649: *RF649 renumbered RF699 in January 1956 (and vice versa).*

RF697: *Converted to a Green Line coach in March 1956 and renumbered RF298.*

RF700: *Delivered in December 1953 fully equipped for driver only operation.*

The Country Bus RFs were the last to be delivered, commencing in March 1953 when RF514 was taken into stock. Internally they were identical to the Central area batch but the most noticeable difference was that they were fitted with platform doors à la Green Line batch. Also missing was the 'roof box' situated above the passenger entrance, the benefits of which, considering the amount of interworking included within Country schedules, was negligible. The delivery of these vehicles was very rapid and all were in stock by the year's end. The first examples entered service from Reigate Garage in March, followed by St Albans (April), Hertford and Hitchin (May), Garston, High Wycombe, Luton and Windsor (June), Leatherhead, Addlestone and Hemel Hempstead (August), and finally Epping and Northfleet (October). This left only a trickle of vehicles to enter stock and these were used to top up allocations at various garages. Even after all had been delivered there still remained a small number of former Green Line 10T10s in use as buses at some garages, mainly in use as peak hour extras. Towards the end of 1953 plans were well advanced for the introduction of 'high capacity' OPO in the Country area using some of the new RF buses. Indeed, RF700 delivered in December 1953 was already fully equipped for such operation. The structural alterations undertaken to the bus to permit driver only operation were quite major and included rebuilding and enlarging the entire driver's cab area. Within this larger cab frame the driver was ensconced with two Ultimate ticket machines and a full size change machine, whilst the cab door carried a glass screen similar to those found at a cinema paybooth. Three further RFs were so treated; these being RFs 517, 647 and 649. RF649 was converted to OPO format after seeing service as a crew vehicle but it is believed that the other two, although delivered as crew buses, never saw service in that mode. Whereas RFs 517, 647 and 700 were available for service by March 1954, RF649 was not converted until the following November. The initial OPO experiment commenced on route 419, operated by Leatherhead Garage, from 3rd March 1954 and was almost immediately considered to be a success. The experiment was transferred to route 316 from 10th August (from that date the 419 reverted to crew operation), operated by Hemel Hempstead Garage. The OPO RFs remained at Hemel Hempstead for some time and it was to be 1956 before any further progress with OPO was apparent.

1956 proved to be a rather hectic year for the RF class generally. A need had been identified for further Green Line coaches and these were to be drawn from both the Central and Country area batches. Furthermore, a decision had been taken to renumber these vehicles so as to retain them within their respective batches. Included within this plan were the four OPO RFs: RF517 took the identity of RF697, whilst 647 and 649 changed identities with 698 and 699 respectively. The purpose of this was to keep the OPO vehicles in their own little batch and all further conversions were to be numbered from 696 downwards. Shortly after the decision was taken that all Country buses would be so converted which rendered this part of the exercise totally pointless! The vehicles chosen to become Green Line coaches were RFs 514–516, 518–532 and 697. These were all treated in March 1956 and were renumbered RFs 295–297, 299–313 and 298 respectively. The Central buses which already held these numbers took the vacant 514–532 series and remained red. This was still not the end however as RFs 533–538 were transferred to Central stock from September to December 1956 and were repainted red in January and February 1958. The reason for this was to solve a Trade Union dispute; more details of which will be found in the Central Bus section. Concurrent with all this was the conversion of a further batch of vehicles suitable for OPO. RFs 684 and 687 appeared from works in February 1956 in this mode. A slightly simpler conversion was implemented by omitting the cab door screens but vehicles all had the enlarged cabs similar to the prototypes. By this time it is believed that the change machine was dispensed with and soon after Ultimate Ticket Machines were obtained with a greater range of fare values, hence obviating the need for two different machines. Between February and July 1956 the whole batch from RF682 to RF696 were converted and these entered service from 11th July 1956 at Amersham, Epping and Hemel Hempstead Garages. So started the spread of Country area OPO which was to be a feature of service alteration programmes for the following three years.

In December 1956, RF664 became the prototype for a further style of OPO conversion. The vehicle retained its original size cab and was simply fitted with a cash tray mounted on a new style cab door which was fitted with a recess to allow the installation of a single ticket machine. An orange plastic 'Pay as you Enter' slipboard replaced the previous inscription which had been mounted at the top of the nearside windscreen (see photographs). All further OPO conversions were to this style, rendering the RF682–700 batch unique. These were hereafter referred to as 'Widecab' conversions and all survived to be taken into London Country stock where they served as a reminder of their earlier pedigree. However, because of the LT overhaul procedure, the bodies were spread far and wide within the Country bus fleet and could be found on the following stock numbers after their last overhaul: viz. RFs 539, 576, 583, 585, 614, 621, 622, 629, 636, 637, 638, 640, 647, 650, 665, 678, 695, 696 and 700. The last 'Widecabs' in service were RFs 614 and 640, operating from Garston and Amersham Garages respectively. Both were delicensed in March 1976, being officially withdrawn a few months later. RF647 was subsequently converted to a tow bus, being finally withdrawn in September 1979.

Following the conversion of RF664, OPO conversions resumed in October 1957, the whole class being so treated by March 1959. Initially some were used as crew vehicles on selected routes even though fully eqipped for OPO. Subsequently spare crew operated coach RFs replaced these buses, allowing them to fulfil their original purpose elsewhere.

The Country Bus RFs from hereon led uneventful lives. Their numbers were increased from the late 1960s when surplus Coach RFs were transferred to the bus fleet, but these retained their coach interiors and could never be classed as thoroughbred buses. The batch of coaches, which had orignally been converted from buses in March 1956, also returned to the bus fold and even though bus style seating had been retained still could not be classed as true Bus RFs.

Apart from a batch of 13 transferred to Central area stock in January 1969 (RFs 545, 563, 570, 580, 590, 598, 602, 603, 608, 617, 627, 632 and 685), the whole fleet was inherited intact by 'London Country' in January 1970. The continung story of the RFs under LCBS ownership can be found commencing on page 67.

The Country Bus RFs were very similar to those delivered for the Central area. The most noticeable difference being that the whole batch were fitted with platform doors from new. No route number roof box was fitted as the amount of interworking inherent in Country Bus schedules would have involved the conductor in a full time job changing the route number plates! RF629 was barely two months old when photographed at Leatherhead Garage in November 1953. *(Geoff Rixon)*

RF548 pauses opposite St Albans Garage on route 391. This particular service was one of those considered busy enough to retain crew operated single deckers until 1969, although by this time the Harpenden section of the route had been transferred on to the 355 and converted to OPO. *(Geoff Rixon)*

Traffic jams did exist in the 1950s, you just had to be in the right place at the right time! Hampton Court on Bank Holiday Monday 1954 proves the point. RF591 operates a relief journey to Kingston whilst on the 604 trolleybus service business appears to be booming. *(Geoff Rixon)*

It was in the Country area that the first experiments with 'high capacity' OPO were carried out. The fact that, in 1954, an RF was classed as high capacity might well cause eyebrows to be raised, but in these humble beginnings was born the first seeds of driver only operation that is taken so much for granted today. Route 419 operated by Leatherhead Garage was converted from 3rd March 1954 and the following August the experiment was transferred to Hemel Hempstead Garage's 316 route. RF517 is seen at Epsom Brettgrave on route 419. This vehicle was later renumbered RF697. *(Alan Cross)*

RF698 (previously 647) is seen at Hemel Hempstead in February 1956 on route 316. *(Gerald Mead)*

A picture which has been seen many times before but no excuses are made for its inclusion in this publication! The cab area of one of the original OPO conversions in 1954. Note the screen between passenger and driver as well as the two separate cash trays.
(London Transport Museum)

The driver's eye view. Two Ultimate Ticket Machines were required along with a change machine seen to the left. Change machines were not perpetuated on future conversions.
(London Transport Museum)

The initial experiments with driver only operation were considered successful enough to embark upon a programme of converting every Country area RF to this type of operation. The first main batch of these conversions took place from July 1956 when Epping, Hertford and Amersham Garages received modified RFs. Seen here is RF686 at Chesham Broadway on route 394B. On these early conversions the 'Pay as you Enter' lettering was placed on the front nearside windscreen at the top and was not particularly prominent. Some time later the familiar orange slipboards made their mark.
(Author's Collection)

A forward facing view of the interior of one of the original OPO vehicles. This style of cab was only applied to RFs 682–700 (see text on page 53) and was referred to as a 'Wide Cab' conversion. No doubt the spacious layout was required to accommodate the change machine!
(London Transport Museum)

RF700 shows the position of the PAYE lettering quite clearly. This particular bus was the prototype OPO conversion and was received into stock fully converted to OPO format. *(Author's Collection)*

Driver only operation spread very rapidly throughout the Country area and undoubtedly was the saviour of many services. RF560 now carries the orange slipboards latterly introduced to signify driver only operation. *(DPR Collection)*

RF656 looks somewhat tarnished in this June 1962 view at Radlett. Overhaul was only two months away however. *(Gerald Mead)*

RF559 prepares to leave Bishops Stortford at the start of its long cross country journey to New Barnet. Few passengers would make the through trip, the cross Hertford facility being more historical than catering for any cross town traffic. Today only a limited service remains and the section of route south of Hertford has long been withdrawn. *(Peter J. Relf)*

The flow of traffic has been reversed since this view was taken in Harlow Bus Station and the RFs and GSs have long since departed. RF644 loads for Sawbridgeworth whilst GS65 scuttles by on the nearside on a Harlow Town Service. *(Alan Cross)*

Inclement weather at St Albans Garage finds RF661 taking on a few hardy souls! One presumes that the destination of the vehicle has been established! *(Ken Harris)*

In 1969 a batch of 13 green RFs were transferred to Central area stock and allocated to Muswell Hill Garage where they ran in green livery for almost six months before receiving the customary coat of red. RF627 waits at Golders Green Station forecourt in March 1969. Originally plans existed for a total of 25 such vehicles to be transferred but in the event no more were to follow. It is thought that had further green liveried arrived they would have been allocated to Sutton Garage for the newly converted 80 and 80A routes but in the event sufficient red examples were scraped up from around the fleet. *(Gerald Mead)*

RF136
AND THE MODERNISED RFs

RF136 appeared from its facelift in March 1966 and almost immediately the decision was taken that a further 174 examples would be similarly treated. The modernisation of 136 did exactly that; so successful was the conversion that it seemed almost impossible to believe that the vehicle was 15 years old. Internally, the decor was very similar to the Routemaster Coaches delivered from 1962 onwards, featuring the same red/grey moquette, new flooring and internal mouldings, and fluorescent lighting. It was externally, however, that the restyling was most apparent. The normal two-piece windscreen was replaced by a curved one-piece example, whilst twin headlamps were fitted— these being in vogue at the time. The traditional livery was applied in a far more striking application. A broad pale green band edged by chrome trim surrounded the whole vehicles and to complement the effect, new style blinds and route sideboards featuring black lettering on a yellow background were introduced. At both front and rear the registration number was lowered and, additionally, revised and improved rear light clusters were fitted. One modification that was not incorporated into the production run was the treatment afforded to the mudguards. RF136 featured round RT style mudguards as opposed to the more square pattern on other RFs. In the event this was not deemed to make that much difference to the general appearance of the vehicle and further conversions retained original style mudguards. RF136 therefore presented a unique appearance and did so for the remainder of its working life.

One interesting fact that does not appear to have been widely documented was the choice of 136's livery. Just prior to the modernisation the new AEC Reliance Coaches (classified RC) for Green Line work were delivered. These featured a startling new livery of Mist Grey with Lincoln Green relief and completely broke away from all that had gone before. It is generally thought that 136 was partially repainted in this style before the traditionalists threw up their hands in horror and as a result the vehicle appeared in more familiar colours. Soon afterwards the RCs themselves succumbed to Lincoln Green and this interesting livery variation was consigned to history.

After the decision to modernise had been taken, treatment of the vehicles concerned was very rapid indeed and by July 1967 the whole batch of 175 had been completed, the last of which being RF63. Initially, the facelifted coaches were not fitted for OPO format but from February 1967 OPO conversion was included as part of the programme. Included in those modernised were the original batch of nine converted for OPO back in 1964 and used from July 1966 on new route 724. This batch were all modernised in April 1967. The tenth vehicle (RF41) escaped modernisation and was reconverted to a bus in July 1967. Twelve of the RFs modernised in April 1967 received additional luggage racks at the rear which reduced their seating capacity to 35. These were intended for use on a new service, subsequently numbered 727, which linked Crawley with Luton via Gatwick and Heathrow Airports hence the need for additional luggage facilities. Seven of the RFs so treated were drawn from the original batch of 1964 OPO conversions (see Appendix B).

By February 1968 all but 25 of the modified RFs had been OPO fitted, and it was at this stage that a conclusion was reached. Too many RFs had been facelifted!

The main reason why there was a surplus of vehicles was quite simply the fact that services had either been reduced or even withdrawn since plans for the original order had been made. Usage of Green Line had been declining for some considerable time and not even the novelty of new Routemasters or Modernised RFs could halt the slide. Traffic congestion was making journeys by Green Line extremely ponderous, not to mention unreliable. Passengers were either taking to their cars or the parallel railways, both of which were considered to be quicker; in the case of private vehicles that was a very debatable point! The decision was therefore taken that the surplus RFs, 25 in number and listed in Appendix B, would be converted to buses and this was undertaken in March and April 1968. The 25 vehicles chosen were those that had not been OPO fitted, although this was done, apart from six vehicles, at bus conversion. The seating capacity was reduced to 37 by removal of the front nearside double seat and its replacement by a luggage pen. Externally the pale green relief band was repainted canary yellow and green, 'London Transport' fleetnames were sited thereon, replacing the 'Green Line' wording. On front and rear the Green Line bullseye was replaced by a yellow and black example proclaiming 'London Transport'. The six RFs that remained crew operated upon bus conversion (RFs 26, 40, 83, 104, 108 and 235) all received OPO fittings two months later in May.

The next stage in our story of the Green Line fleet commences from 1st January 1970 when London Tranport's Country Bus network was transferred to the National Bus Company. The strict rules of standardisation imposed on the RF fleet for its whole life were suddenly swept away under NBC influence, and it was perhaps in the final years of the class's history, at least the green liveried vehicles, that the most interest and variety were found.

For those who wish to know more of the modernised fleet please turn to page 67.

Facing page top: **The prototype modernised RF was RF136 and this appeared in March 1966. Initial allocation was to Tunbridge Wells Garage for use on route 704 and the newly modernised coach is seen here in Chiswick High Road a few days after entering service. Note the RT style mudguards; this feature was not perpetuated on further conversions.** (Author's Collection)

Facing page bottom: **Soon after the evaluation of RF136 the decision was taken to modify a further 174 examples. The first production conversions appearing the following August. Falling traffic on route 715A prompted the allocation of modernised RFs in lieu of Routemasters. First operation was reduced to just Saturdays and peak hours, then to peak hours only. The last day of operation was 14th February 1969 and RF68 at Hertford Car Park illustrates the short-lived allocation of modernised RFs to this service.** (J. G. S. Smith)

GREEN LINE
704 WINDSOR
via VICTORIA
LONDON AIRPORT
GREEN LINE
MLL 523

GREEN LINE
715A LONDON
(MARBLE ARCH)
HERTFORD
715A
LYF 419

Modernised RFs were used to launch new route 727 in May 1967. The vehicles allocated to this service were fitted with additional luggage racks which reduced their seating capacity from 39 to 35. This was considered necessary in view of the fact that both Heathrow and Gatwick Airports were on line of route. Indeed, this fact was always prominent in the extensive marketing of the service. RF66 is seen at Crawley Bus Station. *(Ken Harris)*

The interior of a newly modernised Green Line RF. This particular example carries the additional luggage racks at the rear specified for vehicles intended for route 727. *(London Transport Museum)*

A new style of blind was introduced at about the same time as RF136 appeared and the intention was that it would complement the modernised vehicles. However, RF124 seen here at Harlow Bus Station still carries the former pattern. Harlow Garage was well known for continuing use of the older blinds and the last examples were replaced during early London Country days. *(Author's Collection)*

A limited amount of excursion and private hire work was undertaken by London Transport's Country area during the late 1960s. One such example is this excursion to the 1969 Royal Tournament at Earls Court and RF267 is seen at its destination. *(Ken Harris)*

The practice of operating Green Line vehicles on bus work prior to undertaking Coach Service in the morning peak periods has always been a feature of Country Bus operations. RF77 is seen complete with roof boards, outside the old Longfield Station working a morning peak journey on route 489. *(DPR Collection)*

Enthusiasm for Green Line waned during the late 1960s due primarily to increasing unreliability caused through outside factors. Even as the modernisation programme was drawing to a close came the realisation that too many RFs had been treated. Consequently, 25 examples were downgraded to bus status, receiving yellow relief and London Transport fleetnames. Seating capacity was reduced by two to 37 by the installation of a luggage pen. These vehicles brought improved standards to many local bus routes and RF203 is seen at Sevenoaks Bus Station in its new guise on route 404. *(DPR Collection)*

RF230 was another example similarly treated and is seen here at Hitchin working on the infrequent 386 service. *(DPR Collection)*

LONDON COUNTRY

The formation of the National Bus Company in 1969 and the subsequent transfer of the Country Bus operations of London Transport to this newly-formed nationalised entity probably had far reaching effects on the RF class. Gone overnight were the rigid rules of London Transport standardisation, and it was in the twilight of their careers that the Country RF fleet probably generated the most interest.

London Country Bus Services Ltd, as the newly-formed company was called, inherited a total of 413 RFs. Additionally, five red crew operated RFs were on loan from London Transport and were to remain so for some time. Initial changes were few; the most obvious being the new 'London Country' fleet-name in place of the more traditional 'London Transport'. Over the first few months much carried on as before but behind the scenes plans were being made for the future of the company. Average fleet age was extremely high, indeed the vast majority of the fleet comprised of the RFs and RTs whose age profile dated back to the early 1950s. Almost at once an ambitious programme of vehicle replacement was embarked upon with an eventual aim of fleetwide driver only operation. Management resigned themselves to the fact that in the short-term at least the RF would play a valuable role, being suitable for one man operation and it was decided to commence an overhaul programme comprising the modernised batch. The intention being that these better condition vehicles would eventually replace the Bus RFs which in turn would have been replaced themselves by newer vehicles. Although admirable in itself, due to unforeseen circumstances this plan only partly came to fruition.

During the first two years of London Country's existence changes were few. On the livery front yellow replaced cream as the relief colour whilst yellow fleetnames and numbers appeared in place of the traditional gold. Another visual alteration occurred from February 1971 when certain garages received reduced aperture blinds on their RFs. Blind lengths had always been a problem

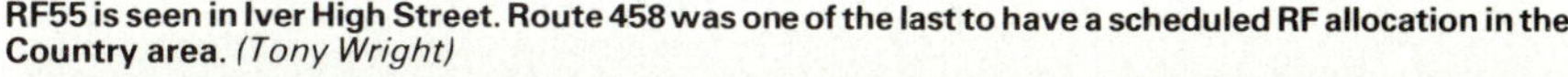

RF55 is seen in Iver High Street. Route 458 was one of the last to have a scheduled RF allocation in the Country area. *(Tony Wright)*

within the Country area as the greater number of interworkings had often created the need for two or more different blind sets at some garages. By reducing the depth of display it was found that all the relevant information could be contained within one blind. Commencing with Amersham in February 1971, garages at Hemel Hempstead, St Albans, Hertford, Harlow and Dunton Green fell foul of this practical but unattractive style of blind.

The new company symbol also appeared during this time. The press release stating: "...the new motif represents the green ring around London in which London Country operate, and naturally suggests the wheel and movement. The angled bars give a feeling of perspective, suggesting operation in depth with a hint of 'transport amidst green fields'."(!) The first RF to carry the motif was RF136 which had found fame previously by being the prototype modernised conversion in 1966.

The five red RFs were all returned off loan, RF393 in November 1970 and the remainder, RFs 325, 341, 374 and 388 the following February. The place being taken by redundant Green Line RFs as a result of service reductions, primarily the part withdrawal of route 710. The first RFs to be withdrawn under the new regime were so treated in August 1971 having been indirectly replaced by newer vehicles or simply made redundant. RFs 86, 197, 557, 572, 573, 575, 600, 628, 633, 635 and 657 being the hapless examples. So started the RF withdrawal programme which although slow to start its peak in the mid 1970s only to be subsequently slowed down by the horrendous vehicle shortage which prevailed from the end of 1973. The intention to retain the modernised examples was maintained and only those which suffered accident or fire damage where the cost of repair could not be justified were withdrawn. The first modernised RF to meet this fate being RF109 in February 1973. Meanwhile the process of converting surplus modernised RFs to buses as undertaken in London Transport days continued. However, whereas LT had reduced the seating capacity to 37 by the installation of a luggage pen, no such modification was undertaken by London Country who were quite satisfied by the simple expedient of repainting the waistband yellow and applying new fleetnames. By September 1973 London Country had painted a total of 61 Green Line RFs to bus livery. The majority also had the roofboard hooks removed but a few did retain this feature and looked a strange sight when subsequently used on Green Line work carrying the boards on their bus livery. Roofboards themselves were also in the process of being phased out, a process which had commenced in January 1973 and was completed by the following summer. The last garage to maintain the traditions of yesteryear in this case being Harlow for route 720.

The Green Line fleet was gradully replaced by new Leyland National buses from February 1973 onwards. The first batch of these vehicles were to standard bus specification with their spartan interiors and poor legroom and were a terrible comedown to what had gone before. It almost appeared that the intention was to kill off the Green Line network and just how many passengers these austere vehicles lost is open to debate. Admittedly Green Line was in decline and it was the result of some fairly major surgery from 1976 onwards that saved the name from extinction, but in the short-term at least a new depth was reached. The reliability of these early Nationals was legendary and this factor at least managed to prolong the reign of the RF on Green Line in the form of substitutions for many months ahead.

One modification which London Country applied to the modernised RFs was the provision of a small vent situated just above the front offside headlight. The sole intention of this was to improve ventilation in the cabs of the modernised examples and it is believed that a prototype conversion was carried out in LT days. However, not all modernised RFs received this vent, the proportion being roughly two-thirds/one-third of vehicles fitted.

The most noticeable change coincidental with London Country ownership was the livery. In LT days green was green and that was that. Admittedly, the seeds had been sown in 1968 to brighten up the livery by the use of yellow instead of cream as the relief colour but this had really only taken effect after the infamous split. As time progressed all manner of different livery variations based on green and yellow took to the streets and a brief summary is contained below.

About mid 1972 some RFs appeared in a lighter shade of green than previous. This was the same colour as carried on the new Atlanteans and Fleetlines that were being delivered at the time. The small number of vehicles so treated were all of the unmodernised type and retained yellow relief and fleetnames, etc. Shortly afterwards the new corporate colour dubbed National Green made its mark. This was a much lighter shade than used hitherto and again was only applied to unmodernised examples. Off white National corporate style fleet-names and numbers were incorporated but the relief colour was no more, everything being covered in a sea of National Green. Some modernised examples did receive repaints although initially at first in standard Lincoln Green. However, a few were painted in the lighter National Green but retained yellow waistbands and very nice they looked too! Of all the liveries that LC RFs carried this was perhaps the most pleasing. Northfleet Garage took things a stage further and three modernised RFs (48, 65 and 88) were painted all-over National Green, waistbands as well; the colour only being broken by the chrome trim around the band. As well as all this there were a few 'one-offs'. RF26, for example, receiving National Green with off white waistband, RF54 retaining Lincoln Green but gaining an off white waistband with a green London Country fleetname. Similarly treated was RF75 which, although Lincoln Green with off white waistband, had the new style London Country fleetname situated on the roof panels. Never before had there been so many livery variations! Even this was not the end of it as when the decision was taken in 1977 to recertify two RFs for further service both received differing styles of livery to what had gone before, RF202, a modernised example, received National Green with off white relief and a roof mounted Green Line fleetname! Considering that the last RFs were scheduled off Green Line work back in 1975 the choice of fleetname was surprising to say the least, but the result was a unique vehicle. Subsequently it was further repainted into traditional Green Line colours and retained, along with the prototype Routemaster Coach, as an official company preserved exhibit. The other recertified RF was 221, one of the former coach to bus conversions in January 1967. This also was repainted in National Green but received off white relief, again making it a unique colour scheme; it carried roof mounted London Country fleetnames.

Another noticeable change which London Country initiated was the treat-ment afforded to RFs 217, 552, 658 and 692 during 1971. In the cases of 217, 552 and 692 the centre front body panel was replaced by that normally fitted to a modernised RF. This in effect led to the removal of the London Transport bullseye filler cap cover which was perhaps the intention. The registration number was also moved to the lower position associated with the modernised batch on RFs 217 and 552 but in the case of 692 retained its original position, albeit on a plate bolted to the front. RF658 featured alterations to the rear lights and registration number, a similar style once again being adopted as on the modernised batch. Quite what the reason was for these mini-rebuilds is unknown. One train of thought is that it was a relatively simple method of removing the LT insignia but here again it had already been decided that the modernised batch would replace the pure Bus RFs at first opportunity. A more logical conclusion could be that it was the result of accident repair damage and that modernised parts were the only type in stock. Either way this small modification quite dramatically changed the appearance of the Bus RFs, for the worst in many people's eyes and thankfully only these four buses were afforded this treatment.

In February 1973, RF204, one of those modernised in the late 60s and fitted with additional luggage racks, was withdrawn due to fire/accident damage. Even at this late stage in the story it was considered necessary for another RF to be similarly converted as a replacement. Resulting from this was the decision to modify RF234 taken. The seating capacity was reduced by four to 35 and the luggage racks from the withdrawn 204 were utilised. The vehicle was allocated to Staines but only lasted until the following January when it too was withdrawn! By this time the need for the 35 seat batch of RFs had diminished and no replacement was authorised. One of this batch was subsequently painted into bus livery and retained its racks; the bus concerned being RF79 which was subsequently allocated to Leatherhead Garage. No doubt the residents of Epsom and Leatherhead appreciated the additional facilities!

Redundant RFs were also converted to service specific needs. For example, RFs 556 and 647, and latterly RF79, were all converted to towing vehicles. Livery applied was grey and yellow and the interiors were stripped out to enable spares to be carried, etc. RF79 somewhat surprisingly was rebuilt at the front featuring an LT bullseye but this was as a result of local indulgence at Leatherhead Garage rather than any change of policy! RF594 was adopted as a recruitment bus and toured the whole system in an attempt to entice staff to join the company. Internally, the vehicle featured such items as desks, loose seats and a waiting area for prospective employees. Standard National Green was chosen for the vehicle's livery but this was later replaced with a brighter scheme employing white as well. At the same time as the change of livery was effected the front panels were replaced with those associated with modernised RFs, in a similar style as on RFs 217, 552 and 692 mentioned above.

Returning to the revenue fleet, as stated earlier, replacement had commenced towards the end of 1971. Although slow to start, momentum increased and by 1974 many examples found themselves laid up with no hope of a revenue earning future. Had events gone according to plan there is no doubt that the Country RF would have been extinct by 1975, but that was without reckoning on the critical vehicle shortage that was to hit the company from the mid 1970s. Many RFs were retained to cover for newer vehicles which were falling by the wayside. Indeed it was a tribute to the soundness of the original design that they were able to do so as some had not seen an overhaul since 1964! From hereon the RF withdrawal programme was dictated by the expiry dates of Certificates of Fitness, although, on paper at least, RFs were gradually being removed from the schedules. By January 1977 the only scheduled RFs were left at Windsor and Garston Garages. Those at Windsor were employed on route 458 with weekend workings on the 446A and 452. Odd Monday-Friday journeys also existed on routes 441 and 484. Those at Garston were employed on route 309. The Windsor allocation was replaced by surplus AEC Swifts from 8th January, whilst those at Garston ran for the last time on 28th January when, from the following day, the service was transferred to Amersham Garage and converted to Bristol LH operation. On paper at least that was the end of Country RF operation. In practice the situation could not have been further from the truth! Part of the 8th January programme had resulted in the total withdrawal of route 335 between Gerrards Cross and Watford as a result of a reduction in County Council support. Chiltern District Council were far from happy with this situation and protested somewhat strongly resulting in the provision of a shuttle service between Gerrards Cross and Little Chalfont until the problem could be resolved. The 'Chalfont Shuttle' as it was termed operated until 26th February when that too was withdrawn. During this brief period the shuttle adopted the 335 route number and was RF operated, this being the last London Country *scheduled* RF operation.

Following on from the January route alterations approximately 20 RFs remained available for service and these survivors were allocated to a variety of garages. Withdrawals, as stated above, were dictated by COF expiry but, in a surprise move, RFs 202 and 221 were recertified in April. By the year's end other than the two recertified examples only four RFs remained licensed for service: RF125 at Windsor, RF175 at Addlestone, RF183 at Staines and RF684 at Chelsham. Of these RFs 125 and 175 expired in January 1978, RF183 in February 1978 (but subsequently resurrected for staff bus duties at Windsor until July 1979) and RF684 in May 1978. Of the recertified examples RF221 was initially allocated to Dartford before moving to Chelsham where a serious defect prematurely terminated its career in March 1979. RF202 was sent to Northfleet where it was used to cover for Bristol LH shortages or for the occasional trip out on Green Line routes 725 or 726.

RF202 is still in stock today, albeit under the auspices of the newly-formed Kentish Bus and Coach Company which was formerly part of the London Country empire. It has been restored to 1960's Green Line livery and often makes appearances at open days and rallies throughout the country.

Until the delivery of new vehicles the RF was the mainstay of many London Country services. Modernised RF134 is seen at Redhill on route 430. *(Steve Fennell)*

London Country inherited 413 RFs and it was perhaps the final years of the class, in the Country area at least, that provided the most interest. Initially much continued as in the past; the most noticeable alteration being the removal of all London Transport insignia and its replacement by the new London Country lettering. Seen here is RF687, complete with new insignia, overtaking RMC1502 (the prototype vehicle to establish the style of the RCLs) in Grays Town Centre. *(Steve Fennell)*

Seen at Grays Garage is RF299 and wrongly registered RT4353. The RT's registration should read NLP518 and not as illustrated. This picture was the result of a staff private hire and shortly afterwards the mistake was rectified. RF299 incidentally being an 'Amersham RF'. *(J. H. Blake)*

Standard Bus RF606 makes a rare appearance on Green Line 724 at St Albans. By this time RFs were no longer scheduled upon this service and this operation was the result of a substitution. However, when such cases arose a former Coach RF was nearly always used. Staines Garage must have been scraping the bottom of the barrel on this occasion. *(Steve Fennell)*

Many RFs were kept on by London Country to cover for newer defective vehicles. One such operation seen here is the use of RF239, a former coach, covering for an AEC Swift in Dartford on route 491 in June 1974. *(Steve Fennell)*

An Amersham RF operating from Amersham. The desire to keep this batch together drifted slightly in LCBS days but a few such vehicles remained at Amersham until withdrawal. RF307 works the schooldays only 332 route (judging by the loadings it appeared to be a non-schoolday anyway!) and is awaiting a driver at Gore Hill, Amersham. *(Steve Fennell)*

Former Coach RF225 is seen at Broxbourne Station. Hertford Garage was one of those to receive reduced aperture destination blinds in 1971 to alleviate the use of different blind sets. They were reasonably legible providing they were set straight and had masking applied correctly.
(Steve Fennell)

Question: When is an Amersham RF not an Amersham RF? Answer: When the body has managed to get itself on a higher stock number. Such were the vagaries of London Transport's overhaul system that such anomalies were not entirely unexpected. The overhauling of bodies and chassis were undertaken independently and the time taken to overhaul these units differed considerably. As a result it was very rare, but not impossible, for the same body and chassis to be reunited when leaving the works. Generally the ruling was that Country Bus, Central Bus and Green Line bodies would not be interchanged outside their respective batches. After the conversion of Green Line coaches to buses commencing from 1962 these rules were still applied, but at overhaul in 1966 RFs 548, 551, 553 and 555 somehow managed to receive former coach bodies, albeit those that had originally been converted from buses to coaches in 1956. This was the only occasion that coach bodies were interchanged and received bus stock numbers. Seen at Orpington Station on the right is RF302, a genuine 'Amersham RF' whilst on the left is impostor RF548. The roof brackets unique to this batch can be clearly seen. *(Steve Fennell)*

As four buses received coach bodies in 1966, so four coaches must have received bus bodies in exchange. RFs 298, 300, 301 and 310 were the vehicles concerned and here we see RF298 at Ware on route 389. Back in 1956, this vehicle was involved in a three way renumbering, hence the fact that the registration carried would be more familiar on RF697. Basically the original 298 was a Central Bus (see page 36) and was renumbered RF517. The original RF517 was one of the first to be converted to OPO format and was renumbered RF697. To complete the triangle RF697 was converted to a Green Line coach and renumbered RF298. At last overhaul 298 received a bus body as carried in this view; confused? *(Peter Graves)*

The modernised RFs in the LCBS fleet were utilised much as before. However, reductions in services and the delivery of newer vehicles rendered many as surplus to requirements and the vast majority were repainted into bus livery and used accordingly. RF162, still carrying full Green Line embellishments, is seen at South Mimms on route 714. The new London Country 'Flying Polo' has replaced the traditional bullseye and fits in quite well on the front panels. Note the addition of a small grille above the offside headlight. This was fitted to improve the ventilation in the cabs of modernised examples and was a London Country modification. Not all modernised RFs received this grille, only about 66% were so treated. *(J. G. S. Smith)*

It didn't take LCBS very long to discard many of the traditions of London Transport. Seen outside Amersham Garage is RF165 on the newly truncated 710 route. No routeboards are carried, presumably as none existed for this now much shorter route. Not surprisingly, the service was totally withdrawn from October 1972. Note also the destination blind; this was the only occasion that a 'lazy display' was ever used on a Green Line route.
(J. G. S. Smith)

Route 708 plays host to RF180 seen arriving at Buckingham Palace Road, Victoria. This particular example has even had its roofboard hooks removed even though it officially is still of coach status. Sideboards were phased out from 1971 onwards and, although a few garages persisted in using them, were extinct by late 1972. *(Steve Fennell)*

As new vehicles were delivered so the redundant modernised RFs found their way on to bus work. RF123 in full Green Line livery is seen leaving Dorking Bus Station on route 439. *(Steve Fennell)*

Plain front panels adorn RF91 as it loads at Welwyn Garden City in May 1974. No attempt was ever made to utilise the new NBC symbol on the vacated area and the modernised RFs remained aesthetically lacking for the rest of their days! *(Steve Fennell)*

ASH WHITE ROAD
490A Southfleet Longfield
LONDON COUNTRY
PAY AS YOU ENTER
PLEASE
LYF 416

COPTHORNE
424
LONDON COUNTRY
PAY AS YOU ENTER
PLEASE
LYF 432

CODICOTE
365 CHILTERN GREEN PETERS GREEN
LONDON COUNTRY
PAY AS YOU ENTER
PLEASE
LYF 419

Facing page top: **London Country reclassified many modernised RFs to buses by the simple expedient of repainting the waistband yellow and applying new fleetnames. In LT days internal alterations were also undertaken but this option did not feature in LCBS plans. RF65 is seen at New Barn in bus livery. Northfleet Garage was one of the first to lose its allocation of standard Bus RFs. All workings being covered by modernised examples.** *(Peter Graves)*

Facing page middle: **A few journeys on double deck route 424 were operated by RFs. RF81 is seen at Copthorne on one such working in November 1973.** *(Steve Fennell)*

Facing page bottom: **The last new route to be introduced which had a scheduled RF allocation was the 365 operated by Luton Garage. This service, which commenced from 4th July 1975, was introduced at short notice following the withdrawal of operations by a local independent. Although only operating three days a week, some journeys were crew operated as spare capacity existed in Luton Garage's crew roster. RF68 is illustrated near Peters Green on the first day of London Country operation.** *(Steve Fennell)*

This page top: **The first noticeable livery change to affect the Country fleet was the repainting of some examples in a slightly lighter shade of green. This colour was not as light as National Green and was similar to that used on newly delivered OPO double deckers at the time. RF561 is seen at High Wycombe once again substituting for a newer vehicle.** *(Steve Fennell)*

This page bottom: **Also repainted in this shade was Stevenage Garage's RF59, seen at Hitchin in April 1974 on route 383.** *(Steve Fennell)*

London Country undertook frontal modifications to some original RFs presumably as a result of accident damage or perhaps to remove the LT bullseye radiator filler panel. The use of modernised RF parts on original RFs produced a most unusual effect as can be seen on this view of RF692 taken at Dartford. On this particular example the registration number remained in its original position.
(Steve Fennell)

RF217 was similarly treated, the only unmodernised original coach so done. In this case the registration number is in the lower position as on modernised vehicles.
(Steve Fennell)

The appearance of RF552 is slightly enhanced by the application of a polo in this view taken in Watford in June 1972. Some five months later the bus was withdrawn, presumably following accident damage as this vehicle was afforded a repaint soon after the date of this photograph.
(Peter Graves)

Following the rejection of London Country's 'mid green' by the National Bus Company, repainted RFs began to appear in corporate National Green. As far as the unmodernised RFs were concerned, everything disappeared beneath a sea of National Green, no relief colour being carried at all. Although fairly smart once outshopped, the colour didn't appear to wear particularly well and in time such vehicles seemed dowdy and very much down at heel. RF611 in the rain at Rickmansworth on route 309 seems to prove the point. Fleetnames and numbers were off white and did nothing to enhance the appearance. Route 309, incidentally, was the last official Country area RF route. *(Steve Fennell)*

'Amersham RF312' had migrated to Harlow by June 1974 and had received its obligatory coat of National Green. It is seen on the short 380 route that was later integrated into the main town service network. *(Steve Fennell)*

RF183 arrives at Staines on route 460. This vehicle was subsequently repainted once more into Lincoln Green by staff at Staines Garage during early 1977. It retained its yellow relief band however. *(Steve Fennell)*

The modernised RFs which were repainted into National Green retained (in the majority of cases) their yellow relief band and very nice they looked too. RF125 appears to have lost half of the blind masking as it leaves Hertford Car Park on route 337. *(Steve Fennell)*

Just because a vehicle was repainted into bus livery didn't mean that it wasn't used on coach service. RF45 seen on route 720 proves the point. Close study of this vehicle shows that the sideboard hooks, made redundant some years earlier, have been retained. *(Steve Fennell)*

Some garages went their own way when undertaking repaints as witness RF48 seen in Gravesend on route 498. Three modernised RFs were repainted in this style by Northfleet, RFs 48, 65 and 88. *(Steve Fennell)*

National Green with white relief was applied to RF26, the only modernised RF to be so treated other than RF202 which again was different by carrying Green Line fleetnames. The bus operated from Crawley, Dorking and St Albans Garages whilst bearing this guise. *(Steve Fennell)*

London Country adopted some RFs as 'service vehicles' after being made redundant from PSV use. RF594 became a 'Recruiting Bus' and toured areas badly affected by staff shortage. It is seen here parked at Hemel Hempstead Bus Station. Business does not appear to be that brisk! *(Steve Fennell)*

RF594 latterly became a 'Staff Employment Unit'. A revised livery was adopted and the front end was rebuilt à la RFs 217, 552, etc. (see page 80). It is pictured at Harlow Garage. *(Steve Fennell)*

Some RFs were adopted as towing vehicles and repainted in a livery of grey and yellow. RF647 is seen at Crawley Bus Station in its new guise. *(Steve Fennell)*

A chance visit to Grays provided this rare photograph of a Tow-Bus in Action. RF556 tows RF286 to its final resting place one Sunday in June 1974. *(Steve Fennell)*

A third tow-bus was RF79, converted in October 1978. Rather surprisingly an LT bullseye was reinstated on the front and gives an idea what the modernised RFs might have looked like had the bullseye been retained. RF79 is seen at Crawley in July 1980. *(Tony Wright)*

THE BEA 1½ DECKERS

The 'deck-and-a-half' coaches supplied to British European Airways in 1952 were a very distant relation of the standard RF. Although owned by BEA, they were driven and maintained by London Transport staff and initially garaged in the basement of Victoria Gillingham Street Garage. The chassis were of the same dimensions as those afforded to the RFW touring coaches. Bodywork was by Park Royal Vehicles and the interior was finished in the same styling as that of a Green Line RF. Initially, an order was placed for 50 vehicles and these were delivered from April 1952 to June 1953. No fleet numbers were carried and the coaches were always identified by their registration numbers MLL713–MLL762. A repeat order for a further 15 coaches was placed and this batch, registered NLP636–NLP650, arrived between August and December 1953. MLL716 was exhibited at the 1952 Commercial Motor Show at Earls Court under the same roof as central red RF330.

The livery first carried by these unusual looking vehicles was BEA's 'house colours' of maroon, off white and grey. A cast crest was situated on the front of the coaches along with two smaller similar examples, one on each side at the commencement of the half deck. Destination blinds were carried with white lettering on a red background. For the first part of their lives these vehicles plied between BEA's South Bank Terminal at Waterloo and the Airports at Heathrow and Northolt. Shortly after their introduction, Northolt was closed as a commercial airfield and all flights were absorbed by Heathrow.

In 1957, the South Bank Terminal closed following the opening of the new West London Air Terminal at Gloucester Road. Concurrent with this opening the BEAs were transferred from Victoria to Shepherds Bush Garage. Round about the same time a new much plainer livery appeared of grey and white. The BEA crest on the front was retained, but those on the side were replaced by a white on orange transfer. During 1960 four vehicles were transferred to Reigate Garage whereupon they took up duties at Gatwick Airport. How long this allocation lasted is not known.

Shepherds Bush Garage was not to remain the home of the remainder of the fleet for very long as from 20th July 1960 the coaches were transferred to the former Hammersmith Trolleybus Depot after its abandonment following stage seven of the trolleybus replacement programme. This was the first time that the vehicles did not have shared accommodation, but even this home was shortlived. A further move took them to the former Chiswick Tram Depot situated in Chiswick High Road. This building is probably better known today as Stamford Brook Garage.

By 1961 BEA was giving serious thought as to what type of vehicle should replace the 1½ deckers. In view of the fact that all maintenance was carried out by London Transport, it was suggested to BEA (by LT) that a coach variant of the Routemaster would be an ideal vehicle for this purpose. BEA remained unconvinced, primarily due to the high purchase price and during 1961 an AEC Regent V was obtained and evaluated. In the event it was the Routemaster that was to effect replacement but not until 1966.

During 1965 BEA's 'house colours' changed once again, this time to blue, black and white and the road fleet changed colours accordingly. The first BEA to be treated was MLL721 and this emerged in a unique livery with two BEA symbols on each side whereas all later repaints only had one. Shortly after this

NLP648, one of the second batch of 'half-deckers', rounds Hammersmith Broadway in April 1957. The vehicle is carrying the original livery of maroon, grey and off white. Note the raised crest on the nearside adjacent to the passenger entrance. An identical crest was carried on the offside and these were removed following repaint into the second livery of grey and white. *(Tony Wright)*

livery was instigated so the new Routemaster fleet commenced delivery and withdrawals of the 1½ deckers commenced. It is thought that not all vehicles were repainted in the blue/black livery and that some met their end still carrying grey and white. The Routemasters generally replaced the half-deckers on a one for one basis but one vehicle was retained ostensibly as a spare to the RMs. This one example (MLL740) lingered on until 1973 during which time it received a further livery variation when BEA once again changed its colours. This time a scheme of orange and white was chosen and MLL740 became the only member of the class to be so liveried. Following withdrawal four half-deckers were obtained by London Transport who converted them into 'Uniform Issue' vehicles. MLL740 was and subsequently acquired for preservation.

Carrying its second colour scheme, MLL753 is seen at Heathrow Airport in June 1962. All of these vehicles were fitted with semaphore indicators when new, the position of which can be clearly seen in this photograph. *(Gerald Mead)*

NLP637 stands at the West London Air Terminal at Gloucester Road. *(Peter J. Relf)*

The third livery carried by these coaches is seen on MLL718 at Heathrow Airport in September 1966. Note that the semaphore indicators have been replaced by something a little more practical!
(Gerald Mead)

The only 'half-decker' to receive the latter day orange livery was MLL740, seen at the West London Air Terminal in September 1970. *(Gerald Mead)*

Two of the BEAs converted to mobile Uniform Issue Units are seen at Chiswick Works in July 1973. The vehicles have been adapted to tow trailers and the type used are those which were originally in BEA ownership for use with the new Routemasters delivered in 1966. *(Alan Cross)*

AFTERSALES

In common with other redundant London Transport vehicles, there has always been a ready secondhand market and this was no exception with the RFs. Initially, the first RFs to be disposed of were the Private Hire batch and various Green Line examples. These were put on the market in 1963 and were soon snapped up for further service; a large number of the coaches being acquired by British European Airways for use at Heathrow Airport on inter-terminal transfers. Following on from this there were very few RFs sold for further service until the early 1970s when redundant London Country vehicles were withdrawn. Prior to that, but after 1963, the only RFs to be disposed of were accident victims or Central area doorless examples, the majority of which went for scrap. This being the reason why so few original crew operated vehicles are preserved today. Many operators stocked up with ex-LCBS examples as it was to be some time before the disposal of the Central area fleet commenced. By this time the novelty of secondhand RFs was beginning to wear off, and in comparison to the Country examples, very few former red buses saw further PSV service.

Private Hire RF5 is seen in Maldon, Essex under the ownership of the well known independent Osbornes of Tollesbury. Note that the front cant window has been panelled over, presumably due to a breakage. *(Gerald Mead)*

Ex-Central RF482 was purchased by the London Borough of Havering for school transport. *(I. Hodge)*

Many of the first coach withdrawals were purchased by BEA. RF275 displays the grey, black and white BEA livery. *(Tony Wright)*

Blue Saloon of Guildford purchased a number of RFs although the majority were of London Country origin. RF389, seen here in a somewhat futuristic livery, is ex-Central area and is one of the 'Uxbridge' batch to boot. Note the single pane doors. *(Tony Wright)*

A considerable number of companies have provided inter-terminal transfer services at Heathrow over the years and for a period of time in the early 1970s RFs belonging to Silverline Coaches were employed. Ex-LCBS RF572 picks up within the confines of Heathrow. *(Gerald Mead)*

Ex-LCBS RF656 shows a more traditional approach to Blue Saloon's livery as it leaves Commercial Road, Guildford on a local service. *(Steve Fennell)*

Appendix A   RF BODY CODES

All RFs were coded by London Transport. Every minor body alteration was given a different code and these are listed below. The code was stamped on to a small plate which was situated on the stair riser.

1RF1/2	Private Hire RF (RF1–25) as originally built.
1RF1/3	Private Hire RF converted to a Green Line Coach (RF16–25).
2RF2	Central Bus. No doors. 41 seats. Crew operated. Originally 289–513.
2RF2/1	Green Line Coach. Doors. 39 seats. Crew operated. Originally 26–288.
2RF2/2	Country Bus. Doors. 41 seats. Crew operated. Originally 514–699.
2RF2/3	Green Line Coach. Doors 40 seats. Crew operated. (Ex-2RF2.)
2RF5	Country Bus. Doors. 39 seats. Fitted for OPO. (Original conversions.) RF700 as delivered.
2RF5/1	Country Bus. Doors. 39 seats. Fitted for OPO. (All those not 2RF5.) Includes Country Buses transferred to Central area in 1969.
2RF5/2	As above. (Difference not known.) 2RF5 (except RF700), 2RF5/1 and 2RF5/2 all converted from 2RF2/2.
2RF5/3	Central Bus. Doors. 39 seats. Fitted for OPO. (Converted from 2RF2.)
2RF5/4	Country Bus. Doors. 38 seats (ran as 40 seater for a short while). Fitted for OPO. (Converted from 2RF2/3.)
2RF5/5	Country Bus. Doors. 37 seats. Fitted for OPO. (Converted from 2RF2/1.)
2RF5/7	Country Bus. Doors. 39 seats. Fitted for OPO. (Converted from 2RF2/1.)*
2RF5/9	Central Bus. Doors (later design). 39 seats. Fitted for OPO. (Converted from 2RF2 from late 1970 for January 1971 Uxbridge scheme.)
2RF5/?	Country Bus. As 2RF5/1. Fitted with Loadmeter equipment. (Sometimes referred to as a 2RF5/7 which duplicates code above.)
5RF2/4	Modernised Coach. Doors. 39 seats. Fitted for OPO.
5RF2/5	Modernised Coach. Doors. 39 seats. Crew operated.
5RF2/6	Modernised Coach. Doors. 35 seats. Fitted for OPO. Luggage racks at rear.
5RF5/8	Modernised Country Bus. Doors. 37 seats. Fitted for OPO. (Converted from 2RF2/4 or 2RF2/5.) A number of 5RF2/4 became buses with London Country but as LC had no use for body codes were not recoded. 39 seats retained.
3RF3	RFW Private Hire Coach.
4RF4	BEA 1½ Deck Airport Coach.

* (Only applied to RF41.)

Appendix B
PH RF GREEN LINE CONVERSION & WITHDRAWAL DATES

RF Bonnet No.	Green Line Conversion Date	Date Last Licensed	Official Withdrawal Date	RF Bonnet No.	Green Line Conversion Date	Date Last Licensed	Official Withdrawal Date
1	–	10/63	12/63	14	–	9/63	12/63
2	–	10/63	12/63	15	–	9/63	12/63
3	–	10/63	12/63	16	5/56	10/62	3/63
4	–	10/63	12/63	17	5/56	11/62	3/63
5	–	10/63	12/63	18	5/56	6/62	3/63
6	–	10/63	12/63	19	5/56	7/62	3/63
7	–	10/63	12/63	20	5/56	8/62	3/63
8	–	11/63	12/63	21	5/56	10/62	3/63
9	–	10/63	12/63	22	5/56	11/62	3/63
10	–	10/63	12/63	23	5/56	8/62	3/63
11	–	9/63	12/63	24	5/56	11/62	3/63
12	–	10/63	12/63	25	5/56	9/62	3/63
13	–	10/63	12/63	All PH RFs were sold between 5/63 & 2/64			

Appendix C   RFW WITHDRAWAL DATES

All RFWs were sold between 9/64 & 1/65

RFW1	10/64	RFW4	11/63	RFW7	10/63	RFW10	10/63	RFW13	10/63
RFW2	10/63	RFW5	9/63	RFW8	10/63	RFW11	10/64	RFW14	10/64
RFW3	10/63	RFW6	10/64	RFW9	10/63	RFW12	10/63	RFW15	10/63

Appendix D GREEN LINE RF MODERNISATION, OPO CONVERSION, BUS CONVERSION & WITHDRAWAL DATES

Bonnet No.	Modern-isation date	Date of OPO conversion	Date of conversion to bus	Date of with-drawal
26	8/66	5/68	3/68	12/75
27	6/67	6/67	3/72	1/75
28	6/67	6/67	–	7/77
29	12/66	2/68	9/71	2/73
30	11/66	12/67	10/71	3/73
31	6/67	6/67	–	7/73
32	4/67	4/67	–	5/74
33	–	10/65	10/65	4/75
34	4/67	7/64	9/71	2/73
35	2/67	2/67	9/71	2/73
36	–	9/65	9/65	3/72
37	6/67	6/67	–	5/74
38	6/67	6/67	–	8/74
39	6/67	6/67	10/72	7/74
40	9/66	5/68	3/68	5/76
41	–	9/65	(9/65) (7/67)**	11/74
42	–	10/65	10/65	6/75
43	6/67	6/67	–	4/74
44	10/66	2/68	11/71	11/72
45	11/66	12/67	10/72	7/76
46	11/66	12/67	4/72	7/73
47	4/67*	4/67	–	7/74
48	10/66	2/68	4/72	2/76
49	11/66	1/68	–	7/75
50	6/67	6/67	3/72	1/76
51	–	5/66	5/66	1/76
52	–	5/66	5/66	4/72
53	1/67	6/67	–	11/74
54	1/67	6/67	††	10/77
55	–	5/66	5/66	1/77
56	9/66	4/68	4/68	3/74
57	10/66	2/68	9/71	2/73
58	–	5/66	5/66	5/73
59	–	10/65	10/65	5/75
60	11/66	12/67	–	7/75
61	10/66	2/68	9/71	2/73
62	10/66	2/68	9/71	8/72
63	7/67	7/67	–	1/74
64	11/66	4/68	4/68	2/76
65	10/66	2/68	4/72	3/76
66	4/67*	7/64	–	1/76
67	10/66	2/68	9/71	4/76
68	6/67	6/67	4/72	1/76
69	–	5/66	5/66	5/76
70	3/67*	3/67	–	8/75
71	–	6/66	6/66	6/73
72	–	6/66	6/66	12/75
73	1/67	6/67	3/72	1/76
74	9/66	3/68	3/68	1/76
75	11/66	1/68	12/73	1/76
76	2/67	2/67	–	7/74
77	2/67	2/67	3/72	7/73
78	1/67	6/67	–	9/74
79	4/67*	4/67	††	10/77§
80	4/67	4/67	7/72	3/75
81	4/67	4/67	2/73	1/76
82	1/67	6/67	2/73	7/73
83	10/66	5/68	3/68	7/75
84	4/67	4/67	10/71	6/75
85	9/66	4/68	4/68	1/76
86	–	2/67	2/67	8/71
87	4/67	4/67	–	7/74
88	2/67	2/67	3/72	7/76
89	4/67*	7/64	–	6/76
90	2/67	2/67	3/72	3/73
91	3/67	3/67	–	3/75
92	–	10/65	10/65	6/75
93	11/66	2/68	9/73	4/75
94	1/67	2/68	–	1/75
95	12/66	2/68	–	1/75
96	–	11/65	11/65	7/72
97	–	–	–	10/64
98	12/66	12/67	–	9/76
99	4/67*	7/64	–	9/74
100	4/67	7/64	–	10/73
101	4/67	7/64	–	10/73
102	2/67	2/67	3/72	6/76
103	10/66	2/68	9/71	6/76
104	10/66	5/68	3/68	10/74
105	12/66	12/67	–	10/73
106	12/66	12/67	–	1/77
107	11/66	1/68	3/72	7/75
108	10/66	5/68	3/68	4/76
109	12/66	12/67	9/71	2/73
110	4/67	7/64	3/72	7/73
111	12/66	12/67	–	11/75
112	4/67	4/67	10/72	6/73
113	–	10/65	10/65	3/72
114	11/66	2/68	3/72	7/73
115	4/67	4/67	3/72	1/75
116	–	9/65	9/65	1/72
117	–	10/65	10/65	3/72
118	1/67	7/67	4/72	10/74
119	12/66	2/68	3/72†	1/76
120	1/67	7/67	3/72	4/77
121	2/67	2/67	–	1/74
122	2/67	2/67	–	1/76
123	3/67	3/67	–	1/76
124	4/67	4/67	3/73	1/74
125	3/67	3/67	††	6/78
126	–	–	–	10/63
127	1/67	1/67	12/73	3/75
128	2/67	2/67	–	12/73

Bonnet No.	Modernisation date	Date of OPO conversion	Date of conversion to bus	Date of withdrawal
129	12/66	12/67	3/72	7/76
130	4/67	4/67	–	1/75
131	3/67	3/67	–	5/72
132	–	–	–	6/64
133	–	9/65	9/65	3/72
134	12/66	2/68	6/72	9/76
135	2/67	2/67	6/72	12/73
136	3/66	2/68	–	12/73
137	–	–	–	10/64
138	4/67*	7/64	–	4/73
139	3/67	3/67	–	10/73
140	3/67	3/67	–	1/77
141	4/67	4/67	–	6/75
142	1/67	12/67	–	6/74
143	5/67	5/67	–	4/74
144	1/67	6/67	–	9/74
145	1/67	7/67	–	11/75
146	5/67	5/67	††	3/77
147	–	–	–	10/64
148	3/67	3/67	–	9/74
149	–	10/65	10/65	9/72
150	2/67	2/67	3/72	1/76
151	4/67	4/67	–	2/75
152	4/67*	4/67	–	4/76
153	11/66	4/68	4/68	1/76
154	11/66	4/68	4/68	2/75
155	4/67	4/67	3/73	6/74
156	1/67	12/67	–	1/75
157	9/66	3/68	3/68	1/74
158	3/67	3/67	–	4/71
159	9/66	3/68	3/68	2/74
160	4/67	4/67	3/73	9/74
161	12/66	4/68	4/68	8/74
162	3/67	3/67	–	1/74
163	3/67	3/67	–	5/73
164	3/67	3/67	–	9/74
165	3/67	3/67	10/72	1/75
166	12/66	4/68	4/68	4/76
167	12/66	3/68	3/68	7/74
168	2/67	2/67	–	5/77
169	11/66	4/68	4/68	1/76
170	1/67	6/67	–	10/73
171	4/67	4/67	–	9/76
172	12/66	12/67	10/72	12/73
173	3/67	3/67	1/73	9/76
174	2/67	2/67	–	2/76
175	4/67*	7/64	–	1/78
176	1/67	1/67	–	4/75
177	10/66	2/68	3/72	1/75
178	1/67	12/67	–	1/75
179	2/67	2/67	–	1/76
180	1/67	1/67	–	1/77
181	11/66	2/68	–	11/74
182	3/67	3/67	–	9/74
183	9/66	4/68	4/68	7/79
184	9/66	3/68	3/68	4/75
185	4/67*	4/67	–	5/77
186	3/67	3/67	–	3/74
187	–	11/66	11/66	1/76
188	–	11/65	11/65	7/72
189	–	12/66	12/66	1/76
190	–	–	–	3/64
191	10/66	2/68	–	1/77
192	9/66	12/67	–	11/72
193	4/67	4/67	–	1/77
194	3/67	3/67	–	11/75
195	4/67*	4/67	–	2/74
196	9/66	3/68	3/68	8/76
197	–	12/66	12/66	8/71
198	2/67	2/67	–	5/74
199	–	9/65	9/65	3/72
200	2/67	2/67	12/73	5/77
201	10/66	2/68	2/73	1/75
202	10/66	4/68	–	–
203	11/66	4/68	4/68	12/73
204	4/67*	7/64	–	1/73
205	3/67	3/67	–	1/73
206	2/67	2/67	2/73	4/74
207	2/67	2/67	–	2/71
208	3/67	3/67	–	2/74
209	3/67	3/67	12/73	6/74
210	–	12/66	12/66	1/74
211	–	–	–	3/64
212	–	11/66	11/66	5/77
213	3/67	3/67	2/73	10/75
214	–	11/66	11/66	4/77
215	11/66	4/68	4/68	12/73
216	–	11/66	11/66	8/73
217	–	12/66	12/66	7/75
218	5/67	5/67	–	8/77
219	12/66	4/68	4/68	11/74
220	–	1/67	1/67	9/74
221	–	1/67	1/67	3/79
222	–	11/66	11/66	5/75
223	3/67	3/67	–	9/76
224	–	–	–	1/64
225	–	12/66	12/66	6/75
226	–	10/65	10/65	7/74
227	–	–	–	1/64
228	3/67	3/67	–	2/71
229	–	11/66	11/66	7/74
230	11/66	3/68	3/68	5/74
231	–	12/66	12/66	9/76
232	–	1/67	1/67	8/71
233	–	11/66	11/66	3/72
234	5/67*	5/67	–	1/74
235	10/66	5/68	3/68	3/75
236	–	1/67	1/67	1/77
237	–	–	–	12/63
238	–	9/65	9/65	10/74
239	–	12/66	12/66	7/78
240	–	11/66	11/66	3/75

Bonnet No.	Modernisation date	Date of OPO conversion	Date of conversion to bus	Date of withdrawal
241	5/67	5/67	2/73	6/74
242	–	11/66	11/66	1/77
243	–	10/65	10/65	4/75
244	6/67	6/67	4/72	1/75
245	5/67	5/67	2/73	7/74
246	5/67	5/67	3/73	6/75
247	–	12/66	12/66	3/77
248	6/67	6/67	–	8/75
249	–	9/65	9/65	12/73
250	5/67	5/67	3/73	10/74
251	–	12/66	12/66	6/77
252	6/67	6/67	3/72	9/74
253	5/67	5/67	2/73	8/74
254	–	1/67	1/67	2/72
255	–	12/66	12/66	1/76
256	–	–	–	12/63
257	–	–	–	5/64
258	–	–	–	4/64
259	2/67	2/67	2/73	3/74
260	–	–	–	12/63
261	5/67	5/67	12/73	2/74
262	–	–	–	3/64
263	6/67	6/67	8/73	9/76
264	–	–	–	5/64
265	–	1/67	1/67	2/74
266	–	–	–	12/63
267	5/67	5/67	3/72	1/76
268	–	–	–	12/63
269	–	11/65	11/65	6/72
270	–	9/65	9/65	3/72
271	–	9/65	9/65	3/72
272	–	–	–	6/64
273	–	–	–	12/63
274	–	10/65	10/65	4/75
275	–	–	–	12/63
276	–	9/65	9/65	4/75
277	–	10/65	10/65	7/75
278	–	11/65	11/65	6/75
279	–	9/65	9/65	3/72
280	–	10/65	10/65	3/72
281	1/67	2/68	–	8/77
282	–	–	–	5/64
283	–	11/65	11/65	10/72
284	–	–	–	6/64
285	–	11/65	11/65	8/75
286	–	9/65	9/65	5/74
287	–	–	–	5/64
288	–	11/65	11/65	10/72
289	–	10/66	10/66	2/75
290	–	10/66	10/66	8/73
291	–	10/66	10/66	9/73
292	–	10/66	10/66	6/75
293	–	10/66	10/66	7/73
294	–	10/66	10/66	2/75
295	–	10/66	10/66	1/75
296	–	10/66	10/66	9/73
297	–	10/66	10/66	9/73
298	–	9/62	9/62	2/73
299	–	9/62	9/62	5/75
300	–	9/62	9/62	7/74
301	–	8/62	8/62	3/75
302	–	9/62	9/62	2/76
303	–	8/62	8/62	7/75
304	–	9/62	9/62	1/76
305	–	9/62	9/62	2/73
306	–	9/62	9/62	9/71
307	–	9/62	9/62	5/75
308	–	9/62	9/62	12/72
309	–	9/62	9/62	1/73
310	–	9/62	9/62	2/76
311	–	8/62	8/62	4/75
312	–	9/62	9/62	1/76
313	–	8/62	8/62	5/73

RFs 289–294 and 295–313 were converted from Central and Country Buses respectively to Green Line Coaches in 3/56. These vehicles had 40 seats instead of the more usual 39. When reconverted to buses the vehicles treated in 10/66 had their seating reduced to 38. However, those reconverted to buses in late 1962 didn't have their seating reduced until 8/63. Of the remainder, if bus conversion took place prior to 1/1/70 then the seating capacity was reduced from 39 to 37. If bus conversion took place during LCBS days (post 1/1/70) then the capacity remained at 39.

  * Signifies a modernised vehicle with 35 seats and additional luggage racks at the rear. RF234 was converted from a 39 seat modernised coach to a 35 seat example in 3/73.

** RF41 was converted from a 39 seat unmodernised coach to a 37 seat bus in 9/65. It was reconverted to a coach in 8/66, being restored to a 39 seater. In 7/67 it was once again demoted to bus status, only this time retaining a 39 seat layout. Internally, it was therefore unique in retaining its original layout when all other unmodernised vehicles were converted to 37 seaters. It retained this layout until withdrawal.

  † RF119 was converted to bus status in 3/72, only to be restored to Green Line condition and livery in 5/72.

†† After 9/73 records of bus conversion were abandoned by LCBS. Many vehicles assumed bus status whilst being repainted at garage level, simply by painting the waistband either white or yellow on modernised examples. It is known that RFs 54, 79, 125 and 146 were, at some stage, repainted into bus livery. RF79 being particularly notable in so much as it was a 35 seater with additional luggage racks.

  § Date shown is date of withdrawal from PSV service. Vehicle subsequently transferred to service fleet.

CENTRAL RF OPO CONVERSION & WITHDRAWAL DATES

RF Bonnet No.	Date of OPO conversion	Date of withdrawal	RF Bonnet No.	Date of OPO conversion	Date of withdrawal
314	7/66	3/79	367	3/65	4/76
315	8/66	7/73	368	5/65	1/77
316	8/66	7/73	369	1/65	3/79
317	8/66	7/73	370	12/70	6/76
318	–	1/71	371	1/71	9/76
319	3/65	6/76	372	–	1/71
320	6/66	7/73	373	–	4/71
321	8/66	2/76	374	–	3/71
322	9/66	11/73	375	3/65	4/76
323	2/65	10/76	376	–	6/70
324	11/70	8/76	377	–	1/71
325	–	3/71	378	–	7/69
326	3/65	4/76	379	1/71	7/76
327	8/66	7/73	380	1/71	11/76
328	8/66	7/73	381	5/65	3/79
329	3/65	3/76	382	7/66	7/73
330	11/70	6/76	383	12/70	9/76
331	8/66	7/73	384	5/65	11/76
332	–	9/68	385	11/70	11/76
333	3/65	4/76	386	–	1/71
334	3/65	5/76	387	5/65	4/77
335	–	4/71	388	–	3/71
336	3/65	5/76	389	1/71	9/76
337	–	1/71	390	1/71	7/76
338	3/65	5/76	391	1/71	7/76
339	–	11/70	392	1/65	1/78
340	3/65	6/76	393	–	1/71
341	–	3/71	394	–	4/71
342	8/66	7/73	395	–	4/71
343	1/65	3/76	396	11/70	8/76
344	–	1/71	397	–	10/68
345	1/71	9/76	398	11/70	5/76
346	12/70	8/78	399	1/65	5/76
347	–	8/66	400	1/71	8/76
348	–	10/70	401	12/70	9/76
349	11/70	9/76	402	12/70	7/76
350	12/70	8/76	403	1/71	6/76
351	1/71	12/76	404	11/70	9/76
352	5/65	10/73	405	–	4/71
353	1/65	2/76	406	11/70	8/76
354	9/66	12/77	407	11/70	6/76
355	12/70	9/76	408	1/65	4/76
356	1/65	4/76	409	11/70	6/76
357	–	9/68	410	–	4/71
358	5/65	1/77	411	6/66	7/73
359	5/65	12/76	412	5/65	4/77
360	1/65	5/76	413	–	4/71
361	–	10/68	414	6/65	8/76
362	9/66	7/73	415	2/65	1/78
363	3/65	9/78	416	–	4/71
364	1/71	3/76	417	3/65	8/76
365	12/70	6/76	418	11/70	10/76
366	3/65	4/76	419	6/65	7/77

RF Bonnet No.	Date of OPO conversion	Date of withdrawal	RF Bonnet No.	Date of OPO conversion	Date of withdrawal
420	1/65	1/77	476	2/65	10/68
421	6/66	11/77	477	–	4/72
422	2/65	10/76	478	9/66	7/73
423	1/65	4/76	479	2/65	12/76
424	2/65	10/76	480	6/66	12/77
425	2/65	1/78	481	3/65	3/79
426	2/65	9/76	482	9/66	10/73
427	3/65	11/76	483	6/65	1/77
428	3/65	3/79	484	–	4/71
429	6/66	4/77	485	3/65	1/78
430	–	6/69	486	6/66	3/79
431	1/65	11/76	487	9/66	9/73
432	6/65	4/77	488	6/66	5/78
433	–	4/71	489	6/66	11/77
434	–	4/71	490	6/66	10/76
435	–	4/71	491	6/66	7/77
436	2/65	6/76	492	2/65	3/79
437	1/65	3/79	493	–	1/71
438	9/66	7/73	494	–	4/71
439	6/66	7/73	495	3/65	4/79*
440	3/65	1/77	496	–	9/70
441	3/65	3/79	497	7/66	7/73
442	3/65	5/77	498	3/65	1/77
443	6/66	4/77	499	3/65	1/77
444	6/66	4/77	500	–	1/71
445	6/66	1/77	501	–	4/71
446	–	4/71	502	3/59	3/79
447	–	4/71	503	3/59	1/77
448	5/66	4/77	504	3/59	3/79
449	4/65	10/76	505	3/59	3/79
450	6/66	4/76	506	4/59	9/77
451	–	4/71	507	3/59	4/79
452	5/66	3/79	508	4/59	4/77
453	5/66	7/77	509	4/59	12/76
454	1/65	4/76	510	4/59	3/79
455	6/65	4/77	511	4/59	3/79
456	9/66	9/73	512	4/59	3/79
457	9/66	6/73	513	4/59	3/77
458	3/65	4/77	514	3/59	7/73
459	1/65	4/77	515	5/59	10/76
460	6/65	1/77	516	4/59	3/79
461	3/65	12/76	517	4/59	4/77
462	5/66	5/78	518	4/59	7/78
463	2/65	9/76	519	4/59	3/77
464	–	6/63	520	4/59	3/79
465	6/66	11/77	521	4/59	4/77
466	–	4/71	522	4/59	3/79
467	–	4/71	523	4/59	11/76
468	1/65	4/76	524	4/59	11/76
469	–	4/71	525	5/59	1/77
470	2/65	4/76	526	5/59	1/77
471	9/66	3/79	527	5/59	6/77
472	2/65	10/76	528	3/59	6/77
473	7/66	7/73	529	5/59	1/77
474	–	4/71	530	4/59	7/77
475	–	5/67	531	4/59	5/77

RF Bonnet No.	Date of OPO conversion	Date of withdrawal	RF Bonnet No.	Date of OPO conversion	Date of withdrawal
532	5/59	4/77	580	3/59	11/73
533	4/59	10/77	590	9/58	10/70
534	4/59	4/77	598	9/58	7/76
535	4/59	9/76	602	9/58	11/76
536	5/59	3/79	603	10/57	8/77
537	5/59	10/78†	608	10/57	3/76
538	5/59	4/78	617	10/57	3/77
545	2/58	9/77	627	10/57	3/77
563	2/59	5/76	632	10/57	10/76
570	2/59	11/73	685	3/56	5/77

RFs 533–538 were transferred to Central area stock from 9/56–12/56. Repainted red from 1/58–2/58.

RFs 545, 563, 570, 580, 590, 598, 602, 603, 608, 617, 627, 632 and 685 were transferred to Central area stock in 1/69. Repainted red from 6/69–7/69. OPO conversion dates given in these cases apply to when bus was green.

RF514–532 were renumbered from RF295–313 in March 1956.

* to LT Museum stock, subsequently sold.

† to LT Museum stock.

RF506 pauses in Cromwell Road, Kingston prior to entering the garage. This part of Kingston is just about recognisable today but redevelopment work has taken its toll. (Author's Collection)

COUNTRY BUS RF OPO CONVERSION & WITHDRAWAL DATES

RF Bonnet No.	Date of OPO conversion	Date of withdrawal	RF Bonnet No.	Date of OPO conversion	Date of withdrawal
539	2/59	2/72	592	9/58	2/75
540	2/59	6/76	593	9/58	10/74
541	2/59	12/72	594	9/58	3/73*
542	1/58	12/75	595	9/58	8/71
543	2/59	9/76	596	9/58	1/76
544	1/58	1/73	597	9/58	1/75
545	2/58	9/77	598	9/58	7/76
546	2/58	3/75	599	9/58	3/75
547	2/59	1/76	600	9/58	8/71
548	2/59	6/76	601	9/58	2/76
549	2/59	1/73	602	9/58	11/76
550	2/58	12/76	603	10/57	8/77
551	2/58	2/73	604	11/57	1/75
552	2/59	11/72	605	11/57	9/71
553	2/59	3/73	606	11/57	4/74
554	2/59	11/76	607	10/57	10/73
555	2/59	2/73	608	11/57	3/76
556	2/59	12/72*	609	11/57	9/73
557	2/59	8/71	610	11/57	1/75
558	2/59	12/72	611	11/57	11/75
559	2/59	1/76	612	11/57	2/73
560	2/59	1/76	613	11/57	3/77
561	2/59	7/75	614	11/57	8/76
562	10/57	2/73	615	11/57	4/76
563	2/59	5/76	616	11/57	2/73
564	2/59	1/76	617	11/57	3/77
565	2/59	10/74	618	11/57	1/75
566	3/59	1/73	619	11/57	1/75
567	2/59	3/77	620	12/57	9/76
568	3/59	2/76	621	12/57	1/76
569	3/59	2/73	622	12/57	7/73
570	2/59	11/73	623	12/57	11/74
571	3/59	3/75	624	12/57	1/75
572	2/59	8/71	625	12/57	1/75
573	2/59	8/71	626	12/57	8/71
574	3/59	8/74	627	12/57	3/77
575	3/59	8/71	628	12/57	8/71
576	2/59	10/74	629	12/57	2/73
577	3/59	2/73	630	8/58	10/71
578	3/59	10/72	631	10/57	10/72
579	3/59	1/73	632	10/57	10/76
580	3/59	11/73	633	10/57	8/71
581	8/58	6/74	634	10/57	10/74
582	8/58	1/75	635	10/57	8/71
583	11/58	1/76	636	10/57	2/73
584	9/58	1/76	637	10/57	2/73
585	12/58	3/73	638	10/57	2/73
586	9/58	1/76	639	10/57	7/74
587	8/58	4/74	640	10/57	3/76
588	9/58	2/75	641	10/57	6/76
589	9/58	12/73	642	10/57	9/71
590	9/58	10/70	643	9/58	9/71
591	9/58	8/71	644	9/58	10/71

RF Bonnet No.	Date of OPO conversion	Date of withdrawal	RF Bonnet No.	Date of OPO conversion	Date of withdrawal
645	9/58	10/71	673	6/58	2/76
646	9/58	7/74	674	6/58	2/75
647	8/58	1/73*	675	6/58	1/76
648	9/58	3/75	676	6/58	3/72
649	9/58	4/72	677	7/58	3/72
650	9/58	2/72	678	6/58	2/72
651	8/58	3/75	679	7/58	3/72
652	9/58	3/72	680	7/58	2/72
653	5/58	12/74	681	7/58	3/72
654	6/58	9/71	682	4/56	10/72
655	6/58	3/77	683	3/56	10/72
656	6/58	9/71	684	2/56	5/78
657	6/58	8/71	685	3/56	5/77
658	7/58	9/71	686	7/56	3/72
659	7/58	8/75	687	2/56	7/75
660	7/58	9/71	688	6/56	12/75
661	7/58	10/71	689	4/56	1/72
662	6/58	9/71	690	5/56	9/77
663	4/58	12/75	691	5/56	9/72
664	12/56	10/71	692	6/56	1/76
665	5/58	7/72	693	6/56	1/72
666	7/58	10/74	694	4/56	6/72
667	5/58	1/76	695	5/56	10/72
668	7/58	12/73	696	6/56	3/73
669	7/58	1/72	697	see below	7/75
670	6/58	6/75	698	see below	7/73
671	9/58	2/75	699	see below	4/72
672	7/58	1/72	700	see below	2/73

The original number series of the Country Bus RFs was from RF514–700.

RFs 514–516, 518–532 were converted to Green Line Coaches in 3/56 and renumbered to RFs 295–297, 299–313 respectively.

RFs 533–538 were transferred to Central area stock from 9/56–12/56 and repainted red from 1/58–2/58.

RFs 517, 647, 649 and 700 were the prototype OPO conversions, being so modified in 1/54 (517 and 647), 11/54 (649) and 12/53 (700). It is believed that RF700 was delivered as an OPO vehicle. These buses were subsequently renumbered RF517 to 697 in 3/56, RF647 to 698 in 1/56, and RF649 to 699 in 1/56. (698 became 647, 699 became 649.)

RF697 was converted to a Green Line Coach in 3/56 and renumbered RF298.

RFs 545, 563, 570, 580, 590, 598, 602, 603, 608, 617, 627, 632 and 685 were transferred to Central area stock in 1/69. Repainted red from 6/69–7/69.

RFs 556 and 647 were converted to towing vehicles in 1/73.

RF594 was converted to a recruiting bus in 8/73.

* Date shown is date of withdrawal from PSV service. Vehicle subsequently transferred to service fleet.

Appendix G ALLOCATIONS OF RED RFs TO COUNTRY GARAGES

The following red RFs were allocated at the dates shown to cover for shortages of green RFs in the Country area. If only one date is shown then the vehicle was only allocated for that month.

RF No.	Garage(s)	From	To	Notes
323	SA	2/66	3/66	
325c	SV	10/69	2/71	On hire to London Country from 1/1/70
326	SA	3/65	7/65	
327	RG	1/67	3/67	
	MA	5/67	—	
	SA	10/67	—	
328	RG	1/67	6/67	
330c	RG	4/65	—	
340	SA	4/65	11/65	
341c	NF	10/69	3/70	On hire to London Country from 1/1/70
	DG	3/70	2/71	
352	MA	10/65	—	
359	MA	10/65	—	
368	MA	10/65	11/65	
370	MA	7/74		Hired to London Country in exchange for Bristol LHS for evaluation
374c	DS	11/69	2/71	On hire to London Country from 1/1/70
387	SA	7/65	9/65	
	RG	12/66	9/67	
388c	EG	10/69	11/70	On hire to London Country from 1/1/70
	CY	11/70	2/71	
393c	GF	10/69	11/70	On hire to London Country from 1/1/70. Towards the finish of hire transferred to Windsor Garage but transfer never officially recorded
408	HH	12/67	1/68	
412	MA	10/65	11/65	
414	RG	10/65	—	
419	RG	10/65	—	
423	RG	10/65	—	
427	RG	10/65	11/65	
438	RG	2/67	1/68	
	SA	1/68	2/68	
455	MA	10/65	11/65	
473	DG	10/66	2/67	
	RG	2/67	6/67	
498	SA	3/65	11/65	
499	SA	4/65	7/65	
506	RG	2/62	10/62	
509	RG	7/59	10/60	
511	SA	4/65	11/65	
514	RG	3/62	10/62	
515	RG	5/62	10/62	
516	MA	5/67	—	
	SA	10/67	—	
517	SA	12/67	—	
526	RG	12/67	—	
528	RG	1/67	3/67	
532	RG	7/59	5/60	
	RG	7/60	10/60	
533	GR	11/65	—	
534	RG	7/59	10/60	

RF No.	Garage(s)	From	To	Notes
535	RG	7/59	10/60	
538	RG	7/59	10/60	

c=Vehicle concerned was a crew bus (no doors, heaters, etc.).

All other loans were used either as crew or OPO buses. Particularly notable are the loans of RFs 509, 532, 534, 535 and 538 in 7/59. This was the first recorded use of red RFs in OPO format. RFs 534, 535 and 538 were painted green until 1/58.

Garage codes:	CY:	Crawley		HH:	Hemel Hempstead
	DG:	Dunton Green		MA:	Amersham
	DS:	Dorking		NF:	Northfleet
	EG:	East Grinstead		RG:	Reigate
	GF:	Guildford		SA:	St Albans
	GR:	Garston		SV:	Stevenage

Appendix H   ALLOCATIONS OF GREEN RFs TO CENTRAL GARAGES

The following green RFs were allocated at the dates shown to cover for shortages of red RFs in the Central area. If only one date is shown then the vehicle was only allocated for that month.

RF No.	Garage(s)	From	To	Notes
33	FW	2/63	5/63	Green Line coach painted in experimental light green
42	FW	3/63	5/63	As RF33
107	T	2/63	3/63	Not known if vehicle allocated for PH or service
291	K	2/61	3/61	40 seat coach converted from bus in 1956
533	SP	12/56	1/58	Repainted red in 1/58
534	SP	12/56	1/58	Repainted red in 1/58
535	SP	12/56	1/58	Repainted red in 1/58
536	SP	12/56	1/58	Repainted red in 1/58
537	SP	9/56	1/58	Repainted red in 1/58
538	SP	12/56	2/58	Repainted red in 2/58
543	K	10/60	1/62	
545	MH	1/69	5/69	Repainted red in 5/69
547	K	11/61	1/62	
550	K	11/61	—	
551	K	10/60	1/62	
552	SP	12/56	1/58	
556	K	11/61	—	
558	SP	9/56	1/58	
560	K	10/61	12/61	
563	SP	9/56	1/58	
	MH	1/69	7/69	Repainted red in 7/69
564	SP	9/56	2/58	
566	K	10/60	2/62	
568	SP	10/56	1/58	
570	MH	1/69	6/69	Repainted red in 6/69
574	K	10/61	1/62	
576	SP	10/56	1/58	
577	K	10/60	8/61	
	K	9/61	2/62	

RF No.	Garage(s)	From	To	Notes
578	SP	10/56	2/58	
579	SP	10/57	1/58	
580	MH	1/69	6/69	Repainted red in 6/69
590	MH	1/69	6/69	Repainted red in 6/69
594	SP	10/56	1/58	
596	SP	10/56	1/58	
598	MH	1/69	7/69	Repainted red in 7/69
602	MH	1/69	7/69	Repainted red in 7/69
603	MH	1/69	6/69	Repainted red in 6/69
608	MH	1/69	7/69	Repainted red in 7/69
617	MH	1/69	6/69	Repainted red in 6/69
619	K	10/60	7/61	
	K	12/61	–	
626	SP	10/56	10/57	
627	MH	1/69	7/69	Repainted red in 7/69
632	MH	1/69	7/69	Repainted red in 7/69
643	K	11/60	3/61	
655	K	10/60	3/61	
	K	10/61	12/61	
674	K	10/60	8/61	
	NB	10/61	2/62	
685	MH	1/69	7/69	Repainted red in 7/69

All loans were used as crew buses.

Garage codes:

FW:	Fulwell
K:	Kingston
MH:	Muswell Hill
NB:	Norbiton
SP:	Sidcup
T:	Leyton

Reigate Garage over a period of time had a considerable number of red RFs on its allocation. RF427 is seen in Reigate on route 447 in October 1965. *(D. Kirk)*